CW01661241

OCR GCSE Religious Studies A World Religion(s)

Christianity

from a Roman Catholic Perspective

Maureen D. Rebbitt · Simon Hughes

Series editor: Janet Dyson
Series consultant: Jon Mayled

Heinemann is an imprint of Pearson Education Limited, a company incorporated in England and Wales, having its registered office at Edinburgh Gate, Harlow, Essex, CM20 2JE. Registered company number: 872828

www.heinemann.co.uk

Heinemann is a registered trademark of Pearson Education Limited

First published 2009

12 11 10 09 08
10 9 8 7 6 5 4 3 2 1

British Library Cataloguing in Publication Data
A catalogue record for this book is available from the British Library

ISBN 978 0 435 50132 7

Edited by Bruce Nicholson
Reviewed by Richard Gray
Proofread by Tracey Smith
Project managed and typeset by Wearset Ltd, Boldon, Tyne and Wear
Original illustrations © Pearson Education 2009
Illustrated by Wearset Ltd
Picture research by Q2AMedia
Cover photo/illustration © tbkmedia.de/Alamy
Printed in Spain by Graficas Estella, S.L.

Acknowledgements
The author and publisher would like to thank the following individuals and organisations for permission to reproduce photographs:

Page 2 Pearson Education Ltd. Tudor Photography. Page 4 Mary Evans Picture Library/Photolibrary. Page 6 Tissot, James Jacques Joseph (1836–1902)/Brooklyn Museum of Art, New York, USA/The Bridgeman Art Library. Page 10 The Gallery Collection/Corbis. Page 13 Lodovico (1555–1619)/Pinacoteca Nazionale, Bologna, Italy/Alinari/The Bridgeman Art Library. Page 14 STR New/Reuters. Page 17 Poodles Rock/Corbis. Page 18 Ryan Pyle/Corbis. Page 20 Arte & Immagini srl/Corbis. Page 22 The Gallery Collection/Corbis. Page 25 Gaudenti Sergio/Corbis Kipa. Page 28 Sacred Destinations. Page 34 Associated Press. Page 41 Linda Kennedy/Alamy. Page 42 Evemilla/Istockphoto. Page 44 Bobby Deal/RealDealPhoto/Shutterstock. Page 46 Christophe Ena/Associated Press. Page 51 David Garry/Istockphoto. Page 52 Ivonne Wierink/Shutterstock. Page 54 Stephen Finn/Shutterstock. Page 56 Atlantide Phototravel/Corbis. Page 62 Alessandro Bianchi/Associated Press. Page 64 Sven Kaestner/Associated Press. Page 68 Associated Press. Page 70 Holger Mette/Dreamstime. Page 73 Bettmann/Corbis. Page 76 Pascal Deloche/Godong/Corbis. Page 80 Dan Forer/Beateworks/Corbis. Page 83B Helene Rogers/Art Directors & Trip Photo Library. Page 83T Libby Welch/Alamy. Page 85 Stephen Finn/Shutterstock. Page 92 P Deliss/Godong/Corbis. Page 94 Ant Clausen/Shutterstock. Page 97 Alex Ramsay/Alamy. Page 96 Ant Clausen/Shutterstock. Page 100 Laurence Gough/Shutterstock. Page 103 Smith & Smith/Dreamstime. Page 104 Elena Ray/Shutterstock. Page 106 Elkor/Istockphoto. Page 114 Pascal Deloche/Godong/Corbis. Page 116 Régis Bossu/Sygma/Corbis. Page 118 Eazign/Istockphoto. Page 120 Ralf-Finn Hestoft/Corbis. Page 122 Glenda M. Powers/Shutterstock. Page 124 Jack Fields/Corbis. Page 126 Rob Stuehrk/Associated Press. Page 128 Terry Healy/Istockphoto. Page 130 Sai Chan/Dreamstime. Page 132 Pascal Deloche/Godong/Corbis. Page 134 Tracy Montana/Corbis. Page 136 Associated Press. Page 142 Sergio Gaudenti/Kipa/Corbis. Page 144 Alexander Kalina/Shutterstock. Page 146 Richard T. Nowitz/Corbis. Page 148 Linda Sladek Garwood/Photographersdirect. Page 150 Colin Underhill/Alamy. Page 152 Burstein Collection/Corbis. Page 154 Mary Evans Picture Library/Alamy. Page 156 Associated Press. Page 160 Arte & Immagini srl/Corbis. Page 162 North Wind Picture Archives/Alamy.

The authors and publisher would like to thank the following for permission to use copyright material:

Bible scripture quotations taken from The Holy Bible, New International Version Anglicised Copyright © 1979, 1984 by International Bible Society. Used by permission of Hodder & Stoughton Publishers, a division of Hachette (UK) Ltd. All rights reserved. 'NIV' is a registered trademark of International Bible Society. UK trademark number 1448790.

To Matthew, with love

Contents

Introduction

A note for teachers

This student book has been written especially to support the OCR Religious Studies Specification A, Units B573: *Christianity from a Roman Catholic Perspective 1* (Core beliefs, Special days and pilgrimage, Major divisions and interpretations) and B574: *Christianity from a Roman Catholic Perspective 2* (Places and forms of worship, Religion in the faith community and the family, Sacred writings). It is part of an overall series covering the OCR Specification A and comprising:

- A series of Student Books covering Christianity, Christianity from a Roman Catholic Perspective, Islam, Judaism, and Perspectives on Christian Ethics – further details on pages viii and ix.
- A series of Teacher Guides: one covering Christianity, Islam and Judaism, and another three covering Buddhism, Hinduism and Sikhism – further details on pages viii and ix.

Who are we?

The people who have planned and contributed to this series of books include teachers, advisers, inspectors, teacher trainers and GCSE examiners, all of whom have specialist knowledge of Religious Studies. For all of us the subject has a real fascination and we believe that good Religious Studies can make a major contribution to developing the skills, insights and understanding people need in today's world. In the initial development of this series, Pamela Draycott lent us her expertise, which we gratefully acknowledge.

Why is Religious Studies an important subject?

We believe that Religious Studies is an important subject because every area of life is touched by issues to do with religion and belief. Following a Religious Studies GCSE course will enable students to study and explore what people believe about God, authority, worship, beliefs, values and truth. Students will have opportunities to engage with questions about why people believe in God and how beliefs can influence many aspects of their lives. Students will also explore why members of a particular religion may believe different things. In lessons students will be expected to think, talk, discuss, question and challenge, reflect on and assess a wide range of questions. As young people growing up in a diverse society studying religion will help them to understand and relate to people whose beliefs, values and viewpoints differ from their own, and help them to deal with issues arising, not only in school, but in the community and workplace.

The study of religion will also help students to make connections with a whole range of other important areas, such as music, literature, art, politics, economics and social issues.

The specification for OCR A Christianity from a Roman Catholic Perspective

The specification outlines the aims and purposes of GCSE and the content to be covered is divided into six different Topics. The book's structure follows these Topic divisions precisely:

Topic 1: Core beliefs

Topic 2: Special days and pilgrimage

Topic 3: Major divisions and interpretations

Topic 4: Places and forms of worship

Topic 5: Religion in the faith community and the family

Topic 6: Sacred writings

The Topics focus on developing skills such as analysis, empathy and evaluation, which will enable students to gain knowledge and understanding of the specified content.

In following this specification students will have the opportunity to study Christianity from a Roman Catholic perspective in depth and will learn about the diversity of the faith and the way in which people who believe in the religion follow its teachings in their everyday lives.

This book covers everything students will need to know for the examination and shows them how to use their knowledge and understanding to answer the questions they will be asked.

Changes to the specification

The specification has changed dramatically according to the developing nature of education and the need for students to meet the demands of the world. The new specification will be taught from September 2009 onwards. The main changes that teachers and students should be aware of include the following:

- The Assessment Objectives (AOs) have changed, with a 50 per cent focus now given to AO1 (Describe, explain and analyse, using knowledge and understanding) and a 50 per cent focus to AO2 (Use evidence and reasoned argument to express and evaluate personal responses, informed insights and differing viewpoints). Previously, the balance was 75 per cent to 25 per cent respectively. There is more information on this on pages x and xi.
- There is an increased focus on learning *from* religion rather than simply learning *about* religion, and explicit reference to religious beliefs is now required in answers marked by Levels of Response.
- Levels of Response grids have been changed to a new range of 0 to 6 marks for AO1 questions and 0–12 marks for AO2 questions. See pages x and xi for the complete grids.
- Quality of Written Communication (QWC) is now only assessed on parts (d) and (e) of each question.
- Beyond the six Topics covered by this book, there is now a greater choice of Topics within the specification including a new Christian Scriptures paper on the Gospels of Mark and Luke, a paper on Muslim texts and a paper on Jewish texts.
- There is also more freedom to study different combinations of religions and Topics.

Why did we want to write these resources?

We feel strongly that there is a need for good classroom resources, which take advantage of the changed Assessment Objectives, and which:

- make the subject lively, interactive and relevant to today's world
- encourage students to talk to each other and work together
- challenge students and encourage them to think in depth in order to reach a high level of critical thinking
- train students to organise their thoughts in writing in a persuasive and structured way, and so prepare them for examination.

The book has many features which contribute towards these goals. **Grade Studio** provides stimulating and realistic exercises to train students in what examiners are looking for and how to meet those expectations. **Exam Café** provides an exciting environment in which students can plan and carry out their revision.

Of course learning is about more than just exams. Throughout the book you will find **Research Notes**, which encourage students to explore beyond the book and beyond the curriculum. All of these features are explained in more detail on the next two pages.

What is in this book?

This student book has the following sections:

- the **Introduction**, which you are reading now
- the six **Topics** covered in the specification
- **Exam Cafe** – an invaluable resource for students studying their GCSE in Religious Studies
- **Glossary** – a reference tool for key terms and words used throughout the book.

Each of the above is covered in more detail in the text below.

The six Topics

Each Topic in this book contains:

- a Topic scene-setter (**The Big Picture**)
- a look at the key questions raised by the Topic, and the key words and issues associated with those questions (**Develop your knowledge**)
- two-page spreads covering the **main Topic content**
- two pages of different level questions to check understanding of the Topic material (**Remember and Reflect**)
- exam-style questions with level indicators, examiner's comments and model answers (**Grade Studio**).

These features, which are explained more fully in the following pages, have been carefully planned and designed to draw together the OCR specification in an exciting but manageable way.

The Big Picture

This provides an overview of the Topic. It explains to students **what** they will be studying (the content), **how** they will study it (the approaches, activities and tasks) and **why** they are studying it (the rationale). It also includes a **Get started** activity, often linked to a picture or visual stimuli, which presents a task designed to engage students in the issues of the Topic and give them some idea of the content to be studied.

Develop your knowledge

This lists the **key information**, **key questions** and **key words** of the Topic. At a glance, it allows students to grasp the basic elements of knowledge they will gain in the study of the Topic. It is also a useful reference point for reflection and checking information as it is studied.

Main Topic content

The main content of each Topic is covered in a number of two-page spreads. Each spread equates to roughly one lesson of work – although teachers will need to judge for themselves if some of these need more time.

Each spread begins with the learning outcomes, highlighted in a box at the top of the page, so that students are aware of the focus and aims of the lesson. The text then attempts to answer, from a balanced viewpoint, one or two of the key questions raised in

Develop your knowledge. The text carefully covers the views of both religious believers and non-believers. It is also punctuated with activities that range from simple tasks that can take place in the classroom to more complex tasks that can be tackled away from school.

A range of margin features adds extra depth and support to the main text both for students and the teacher.

- **For debate** invites students to examine two sides of a controversial issue.
- **Must think about!** directs students towards a key idea that they should consider.
- **Sacred text** provides an extract from one of the religions covered in the Topic to help students understand religious ideas and teachings.
- **Research notes** provides stimulating ideas for further research beyond the material covered in the book and in the OCR specification.

Activities

Every Topic has a range of interesting activities which will help students to achieve the learning outcomes. Every two-page spread has a short starter activity to grab students' attention and to get them thinking (see **Get Started** activity on page vi). This is followed by a development section where the main content is introduced, and a plenary activity, which may ask students to reflect on what they have learnt, or may start them thinking about the next steps.

All activities are labelled AO1 or AO2 so you can tell at a glance which skills will be developed.

Remember and Reflect

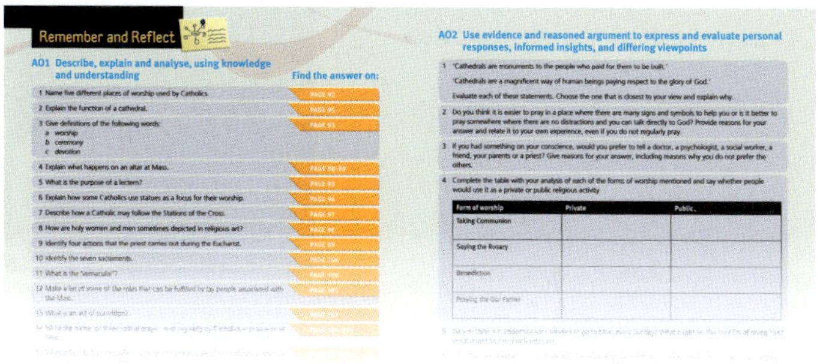

This provides an opportunity for students to reflect on what they have learned and identify possible weaknesses or gaps in their knowledge. It also helps them to recognise key ideas in the specification content. Once they have tested their knowledge with the first set of questions, a cross-reference takes them back to the relevant part of the text so they can check their answers. A second set of questions helps them to develop the AO2 skills necessary for the examination.

What is Grade Studio?

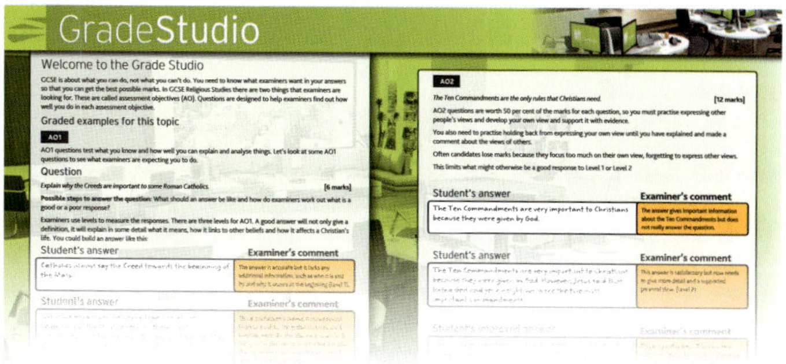

Everyone has different learning needs and this section of the book gives clear focus on how, with guidance from the teacher, students can develop the skills that will help them to achieve the higher levels in their exam responses.

Grade Studio appears as boxes within each Topic, as well as a two-page spread at the end of every Topic. It includes tips from the examiner, guidance on the steps to completing a well structured answer, and sample answers with examiner comments.

What is the Exam Café?

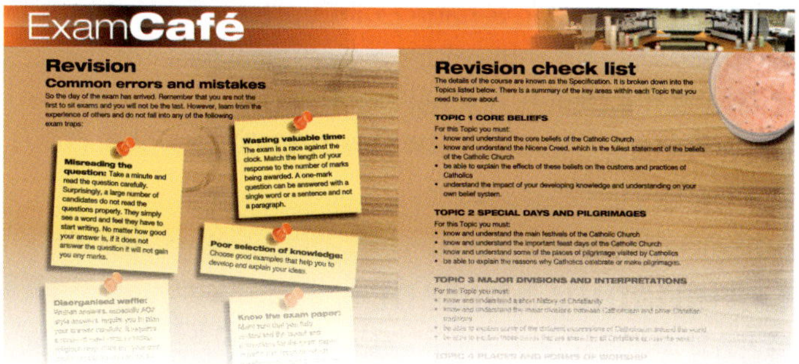

This is the revision section of the book. Here students will find useful revision tools and tips on how to get started on their revision and exam preparation. Students will also find assessment advice, including examples of different types of questions and samples of frequently asked questions. A useful **revision check list** allows students to review each Topic's content and explains where to find material in the book that relates to the exam questions.

Exam Café also has:

- sample student answers with examiner's comments
- help on understanding exam language, so students can achieve higher grades
- examiner tips, including common mistakes to be avoided.

Heinemann's OCR Religious Studies A Series

Perspectives on Christian Ethics Student Book

ISBN 978-0-435-50270-6

This book provides complete coverage of both units of Christian Ethics (B589 and B603). It provides information, activities, and Grade Studio examples for all aspects of the course, as well as an 8-page Exam Café for revision. Teachers will find support for almost all aspects of this course in the OCR B Teacher Guide: Philosophy and Applied Ethics (ISBN 978-0-435-50152-5).

Islam Student Book

ISBN 978-0-435-50134-1

This book provides complete coverage of both units of Islam (B577 and B578). It provides information, activities, and Grade Studio examples for all aspects of the course, as well as an 8-page Exam Café for revision. Comprehensive support for the Teacher is provided through the corresponding OCR A Teacher Guide (see below).

Christianity Student Book

ISBN 978-0-435-50130-3

This book provides complete coverage of both units of Christianity (B571 and B572). It provides information, activities, and Grade Studio examples for all aspects of the course, as well as an 8-page Exam Café for revision. Comprehensive support for the Teacher is provided through the corresponding OCR A Teacher Guide (see below).

Judaism Student Book

ISBN 978-0-435-50133-4

This book provides complete coverage of both units of Judaism (B579 and B580). It provides information, activities, and Grade Studio examples for all aspects of the course, as well as an 8-page Exam Café for revision. Comprehensive support for the Teacher is provided through the corresponding OCR A Teacher Guide (see below).

OCR A Teacher Guide – Christianity, Islam and Judaism, with editable CD-ROM

ISBN 978-0-435-50136-5

This Teacher Guide covers Christianity, Islam and Judaism. It corresponds throughout to the Student Books and contains lesson plans, worksheets and Grade Studios to provide a complete teaching course for the chosen religion(s). The Christianity section of the Teacher Guide covers each Topic in the specification with six sample lesson plans and worksheets. The other religions have three sample lesson plans and worksheets. Everything is cross-referenced to the student books to help you make the most out of these resources.

The Teacher Guide comes with an editable CD-ROM, which contains all the lesson plans along with a fully customisable version of all the worksheets.

OCR A Teacher Guide – Buddhism

ISBN 978-0-435-50129-7

This Teacher Guide covers Buddhism. It contains lesson plans, worksheets and Grade Studios to provide a complete teaching course for Buddhism. It covers Units B569 and B570 in the OCR A specification.

OCR A Teacher Guide – Hinduism

ISBN 978-0-435-50128-0

This Teacher Guide covers Hinduism. It contains lesson plans, worksheets and Grade Studios to provide a complete teaching course for Hinduism. It covers Units B575 and B576 in the OCR A specification.

OCR A Teacher Guide – Sikhism

ISBN 978-0-435-50127-3

This Teacher Guide covers Sikhism. It contains lesson plans, worksheets and Grade Studios to provide a complete teaching course for Sikhism. It covers Units B581 and B582 in the OCR A specification.

Assessment Objectives and Levels of Response

Assessment Objectives, AO1 and AO2

In the new specification, the questions in the examination are designed to test students against two Assessment Objectives: AO1 and AO2. In the specification 50 per cent of the marks will be awarded for AO1 questions and 50 per cent will be awarded for AO2 questions.

AO1 Questions require candidates to 'describe, explain and analyse, using knowledge and understanding'.

AO2 Questions require candidates to 'use evidence and reasoned argument to express and evaluate personal responses, informed insights, and differing viewpoints'.

Each question in the examination is composed of 5 parts, **a–e**. In more detail:

- Parts **a–c** are worth one, two and three marks respectively and test a candidate's knowledge (AO1 skills).
- Part **d** is worth six marks and tests a candidate's understanding (AO1 skills).
- Part **e** is worth twelve marks and tests a candidate's AO2 skills.

LEVELS OF RESPONSE FOR MARKING AO1 PART (D) QUESTIONS

LEVEL 1

(1–2 marks)

A **weak** attempt to answer the question.

Candidates will demonstrate little understanding of the question.

- A small amount of relevant information may be included.
- Answers may be in the form of a list with little or no description/explanation/analysis.
- There will be little or no use of specialist terms.
- Answers may be ambiguous or disorganised.
- Errors of grammar, punctuation and spelling may be intrusive.

LEVEL 2

(3–4 marks)

A **satisfactory** answer to the question.

Candidates will demonstrate some understanding of the question.

- Information will be relevant but may lack specific detail.
- There will be some description/explanation/analysis although this may not be fully developed.
- The information will be presented for the most part in a structured format.
- Some use of specialist terms, although these may not always be used appropriately.
- There may be errors in spelling, grammar and punctuation.

LEVEL 3

(5–6 marks)

A **good** answer to the question.

Candidates will demonstrate a clear understanding of the question.

- A fairly complete and full description/explanation/analysis.
- A comprehensive account of the range and depth of relevant material.
- The information will be presented in a structured format.
- There will be significant, appropriate and correct use of specialist terms.
- There will be few, if any, errors in spelling, grammar and punctuation.

LEVELS OF RESPONSE FOR MARKING AO2 PART (E) QUESTIONS

LEVEL 0 (0 marks)	**No evidence submitted or response does not address the question.**
LEVEL 1 (1–3 marks)	A **weak** attempt to answer the question. Candidates will demonstrate little understanding of the question. • Answers may be simplistic with little or no relevant information. • Viewpoints may not be supported or appropriate. • Answers may be ambiguous or disorganised. • There will be little or no use of specialist terms. • Errors of grammar, punctuation and spelling may be intrusive.
LEVEL 2 (4–6 marks)	A **limited** answer to the question. Candidates will demonstrate some understanding of the question. • Some information will be relevant, although may lack specific detail. • Only one view might be offered and developed. • Viewpoints might be stated and supported with limited argument/discussion. • The information will show some organisation. • Reference to the religion studied may be vague. • Some use of specialist terms, although these may not always be used appropriately. • There may be errors in spelling, grammar and punctuation.
LEVEL 3 (7–9 marks)	A **competent** answer to the question. Candidates will demonstrate a sound understanding of the question. • Selection of relevant material with appropriate development. • Evidence of appropriate personal response. • Justified arguments/different points of view supported by some discussion. • The information will be presented in a structured format. • Some appropriate reference to the religion studied. • Specialist terms will be used appropriately and for the most part correctly. • There may be occasional errors in spelling, grammar and punctuation.
LEVEL 4 (10–12 marks)	A **good** answer to the question. Candidates will demonstrate a clear understanding of the question. • Answers will reflect the significance of the issue(s) raised. • Clear evidence of an appropriate personal response, fully supported. • A range of points of view supported by justified arguments/discussion. • The information will be presented in a clear and organised way. • Clear reference to the religion studied. • Specialist terms will be used appropriately and correctly. • Few, if any, errors in spelling, grammar and punctuation.

Topic 1: Core beliefs

The Big Picture

In this Topic you will be examining:

- the core beliefs of the Catholic Church
- the Nicene Creed as the fullest statement of the beliefs of Catholics
- the effects of these beliefs on the customs and practices of Catholics
- the impact of your developing knowledge and understanding on your own belief system.

What?

You will:

- look at the Creed and other statements of Catholic belief
- study the central beliefs of Catholics
- examine official Church teaching on these matters of faith.

Why?

Because:

- knowing what Catholics believe can help us to understand their religious practices
- understanding the underpinning beliefs of Catholics aids understanding of the way they act and behave
- knowing and understanding the core beliefs of Catholics can act as a powerful way of understanding your own belief system.

How?

By:

- reading the Nicene Creed
- examining each clause in the Creed and extracting its theological meaning
- looking at the impact of beliefs on the rituals and religious practices of the Catholic Church
- comparing Catholic beliefs with the things you hold to be important and true
- analysing how people come to know what is true, valid and authentic.

The mass is the central act of Catholic worship.

GET STARTED

On a piece of paper write down the ten things that are most important to you. They can be anything you like but they must be things to which you feel a sense of emotional attachment. Now ask yourself the following questions:

- Would you be prepared to risk your own life for any of those beliefs?
- Would you find it embarrassing to share any of those beliefs with members of your class?
- Do your parents or carers know that you hold these beliefs?

Develop your knowledge

Core beliefs

KEY INFORMATION

- The Nicene Creed is a full statement of Catholic beliefs.
- The Nicene Creed is shared with all Christians as a central statement of the faith.
- The Church decided on this creed in 325 CE at the Council of Nicaea.
- For Catholics, there is one God in three persons – the Trinity.
- For Catholics, Jesus is the human and most visible form of the Trinity.
- The beliefs of Catholics are decided by councils of the Church and are guarded by the teaching authority of the Church (the Magisterium).
- The Sacred Congregation for the Doctrine of the Faith is the Vatican body that oversees the Church's teaching.
- Most articles of the Catholic faith never change, but some are shifted by advances in human knowledge and understanding.

The First Council of Nicaea 325 CE.

KEY QUESTIONS

KNOWLEDGE AND UNDERSTANDING

What do Catholics believe?

How do these beliefs differ from those of other Christians?

ANALYSIS AND EVALUATION

Which aspects of your own belief system coincide with the teachings of the Catholic Church and the beliefs of its adherents?

Can you find justification for your beliefs and provide evidence to support them?

KEY WORDS

apostle One of the twelve of Jesus' closest disciples. 'Apostle' means 'one who is sent' and is the name given, therefore, to those who were sent out by Jesus to preach, to baptise and to gather the people into the Church.

Roman Catholic A member of the Church of Rome (the word 'catholic' also means 'universal').

Christ The Anointed One.

Christian A believer in and follower of Jesus.

Church The word has three meanings: (i) the building where Christians worship, (ii) the congregation who worship in that building and who go out into the world to serve Jesus, and (iii) the fellowship of all believers.

creed A statement of beliefs.

Father One person of the threefold nature of God; one of the Trinity.

gospels The four books found in the New Testament that relate the stories of Jesus in his life on Earth.

Heaven The place, or state, in which souls will be united with God after death.

Hell The place, or state, in which souls will be separated from God after death.

Holy Spirit One person of the threefold nature of God; one of the Trinity.

incarnation The doctrine that God took human form in Jesus Christ.

Jesus of Nazareth The central figure of Christian history and devotion. The second person of the Trinity.

Lord Title used for Jesus to express his divine lordship over people, time and space.

Mary The Virgin Mary, Mother of Christ, Mother of God.

Messiah Used in the Jewish tradition to refer to the expected leader sent by God, who will bring salvation to God's people.

New Testament Collection of 27 books forming the second section of the Canon of Christian Scriptures.

Old Testament That part of the Christian Scriptures which the Church shares with Judaism, comprising 39 books covering the Hebrew Canon (and in the case of certain denominations, some additional books).

Original Sin The general condition of sinfulness, or lack of holiness, into which human beings are born, arising from the sin of Adam and Eve in the garden of Eden.

Purgatory In Roman Catholic teaching, a place where souls may go after death to be cleansed from sin and prepared for heaven.

resurrection The belief that Christ rose from the dead after his execution.

sin An act of rebellion against the known will of God.

Son One person of the threefold nature of God; one of the Trinity.

Trinity Three persons in one God; doctrine of the threefold nature of God – Father, Son and Holy Spirit.

Virgin Birth The doctrine of the miraculous conception of Jesus Christ by the Virgin Mary through the power of the Holy Spirit and without the agency of a human father.

FOR INTEREST

The Vatican City is a walled area inside the city of Rome (Italy's capital). It covers 110 acres and has a population of around 800. This makes it the smallest country in the world both by population and area. The ruler of the Vatican City is the Pope.

Creed

The next two pages will help you to:

- distinguish between the Nicene Creed and other statements of Catholic belief
- explain the origins of the Creeds and their purpose in the Church
- evaluate some of the core beliefs of the Catholic Church and compare them with your own set of values.

And Jesus said to them, 'Come after me and I will make you into fishers of people.' (Mark 1:17)

Getting started with Catholic belief

An early symbol of Christianity is the fish. Some of the first disciples were fishermen and when **Jesus** called them he told them they would be 'fishers of people' (Mark 1:16–20). In Greek the word 'fish' is 'ichthus'. Ichthus is an acronym. Each letter is the first letter of the Greek words which makes up the statement of faith: Jesus **Christ** God's **Son** Saviour.

Persecuted early **Christians**, trying to avoid detection, would sketch the outline of a fish in the sand. Other passing Christians would place their staff in the drawing as if it were the eye of the fish. In code, they were saying 'I see things your way too.'

This is an example of an early **creed**. Other statements include the Lord's Prayer which was said by Christians together as they prayed in secret.

The one statement that unites all Christians is 'Jesus Christ My Lord and Saviour'. It is a simple statement but behind it is a great deal of meaning.

AO1 skills ACTIVITIES

Christian creeds set out the main beliefs of the Christian religion. Compare and contrast the statements made in the Apostles' and the Nicene Creeds. Briefly explain the similarities and the differences.

The purpose of beliefs

The early **Church** realised that it was important to have an agreed unified set of beliefs. At the First Council of Nicaea, held in 325 CE, the Church created a Creed which set out all their core beliefs and which could be accepted by all Christians. The word 'creed' comes from the Latin for 'I believe'. The Nicene Creed was then adopted by the Council of Constantinople in 381 CE. It was partly created as a reaction to the Arian belief that Jesus was wholly divine and not human.

Nicene Creed – Missal

We believe in one God, the Father, the Almighty, maker of heaven and earth, of all that is, seen and unseen.
We believe in one Lord, Jesus Christ, the only Son of God, eternally begotten of the Father, God from God, Light from Light, true God from true God, begotten, not made, of one Being with the Father. Through him all things were made. For us men and for our salvation he came down from heaven: by the power of the Holy Spirit he became incarnate from the Virgin Mary, and was made man. For our sake he was crucified under Pontius Pilate; he suffered death and was buried. On the third day he rose again in accordance with the Scriptures; he ascended into heaven and is seated at the right hand of the Father.
He will come again his glory to judge the living and the dead, and his kingdom will have no end.
We believe in the Holy Spirit, the Lord, the giver of life, who proceeds from the Father and the Son. With the Father and the Son he is worshipped and glorified. He has spoken through the Prophets. We believe in one holy catholic and apostolic Church. We acknowledge one baptism for the forgiveness of sins. We look for the resurrection of the dead, and the life of the world to come. Amen.

Other creeds

Catholics say the Nicene Creed at Mass on Sundays, but there are other creeds. Another important creed is the Apostles' Creed. It is so named because legend has it that each of the Twelve **apostle**s wrote a part of it. As a result, it is divided into twelve parts.

The Apostles' Creed

I believe in God, the Father almighty, creator of heaven and earth.
I believe in Jesus Christ, his only Son, our Lord.
He was conceived by the power of the Holy Spirit and born of the Virgin Mary.
He suffered under Pontius Pilate, was crucified, died, and was buried.
He descended to the dead. On the third day he rose again.
He ascended into heaven and is seated at the right hand of the Father.
He will come again to judge the living and the dead.
I believe in the Holy Spirit,
the holy catholic Church, the communion of saints,
the forgiveness of sins,
the resurrection of the body,
and the life everlasting.
Amen.

AO2 skills ACTIVITIES

Which of the two creeds on these pages do you find more clearly expresses to you the beliefs of Catholics? Which bits don't you understand? How could you find out what each individual article means? (An article is each statement, usually a line of text.)

Examine the idea that no one creed can contain all truth. What arguments would you use to support and challenge this position?

The Holy Trinity

The next two pages will help you to:

- examine the doctrine of the Trinity
- explore the Catholic approach to the Trinity
- evaluate the nature of the Trinity as you understand it.

Three persons in one

The doctrine of the **Trinity** is one of the most complex ideas in Christianity and there are differences of opinion about it. The three persons of the Trinity are God the **Father**, God in the human form of **Jesus** and God in the form of the **Holy Spirit**. St Patrick is said to have likened the Trinity to a three-leaved clover – the shamrock. Each leaf is unique and exists on its own but it shares the same substance as the others. Nowadays it could be said that it is genetically the same even if its appearance varies from leaf to leaf.

Others have said the Trinity is like the chemical compound H_2O, which exists as liquid water, steam and ice. This is quite a neat metaphor, especially if ice is equated to the physical presence of H_2O in the world. This is the function Jesus performs for the Trinity. Steam could be equated to a formless object just like a spirit, and water itself is the very essence of existence. Without water nothing living can survive, which is a perfect way of expressing **Catholic** belief about God.

AO1 skills ACTIVITIES

Draw and label a symbol of the Trinity. Consider with your work partner how effective this symbol is.

One substance, different functions

Each part of the Trinity has a particular function to carry out. God is seen by Catholics as the creator and sustainer of the Universe. Jesus is seen as the human face of God, who makes God accessible and known. The Holy Spirit is the presence of God in the world today. Each part of the Trinity has equal status in Catholic belief. The Trinity could be represented as shown in the diagram.

Worship of the Trinity

The Holy Trinity is celebrated on Trinity Sunday, the week after Pentecost. By celebrating it at that time, the **Church** is acknowledging the arrival of the Holy Spirit and the courage and strength it gave to the **apostles**.

The mystery of the Trinity

Some **Christian** denominations do not have the same view of the Trinity as Catholics do. For example, Unitarians do not believe in the Trinity and teach the absolute importance of God the Father alone. Alternatively, Jehovah's Witnesses do not believe that Jesus is eternal, citing the text in Colossians which says that Jesus was the first-born of all creation (Colossians 1:15). In other words, God made Jesus, so he cannot be equal to God. Catholics see these two contrasting positions as heretical (inconsistent with official Church doctrine).

The symbol of the Unitarian Church.

FOR INTEREST

The Charismatic renewal movement in the Catholic Church took much of its inspiration from the Greek word 'charisma' which means 'spirit' or 'gift'. If someone is described as charismatic, it is usually because they have a great spirit that people can recognise. In the Bible, Jesus is often recognised just from the spirit that flows out of him.

AO2 skills ACTIVITIES

Catholics find it difficult to explain their belief in the Trinity, but they know that it is true. Assemble the case which convinces them that the Trinity is true and examine the strengths and weaknesses of the evidence.

If you were a radio presenter, what questions would you like to put to the three members of the Holy Trinity to help Catholics understand the different roles they play and how God the Father, God the Son and God the Holy Spirit can be separate yet united?

God

Michaelangelo's painting of the 'Creation of Adam', on the ceiling of the Sistine Chapel in the Vatican City, Italy..

The next two pages will help you to:

- describe the attributes of God
- explain some of the complex concepts that support Catholic beliefs about God
- present your own beliefs about God, with evidence to support your opinion.

God the Father

The creative force of the Universe is known to **Catholics** as God. Catholics always write his name with a capital G so as to reinforce their view that there is only one God, the maker of all things. God is often referred to as the Creator because of this. Catholics believe that nothing exists unless God created it and believe that God created the world out of nothing (*ex nihilo* in Latin). Catholics are not opposed to the idea of the Big Bang and agree with scientists that the evidence from science is that God took a very long time to create the world that is still evolving to this day.

AO1 skills **ACTIVITIES**

Explain how God is described in the Nicene Creed or the Apostles' Creed. Give reasons why you think there is so little written about God in contrast to the sections on Jesus.

God is called '**Father**' in the Nicene **Creed** to signify this creative force. Fatherhood, in human terms, is about reproductive activity and the generation of new life. This is one of the ways in which Catholics view God.

Omniscience

Catholics believe that God knows everything. He created the world, so he knows what is in it and what is going to happen. This attribute of God is called *omniscience* from the Latin word for 'all-knowing'. According to Catholic belief, God can even see things that are unseen by humans. The prophet Jeremiah said that God knew people in the womb even before they were born.

Omnipotence

Omnipotence is the word used to describe the power that God has to do whatever he chooses. Catholic belief is that there is nothing that God cannot do. The word omnipotence comes from the Latin word for 'all-powerful'. In the **Old Testament** there are stories of God parting the sea, creating a pillar of fire, causing storms, sending plagues of locusts, boils and sickness. In the **New Testament**, God is revealed through the power of **Jesus**. The big question for Catholics is whether or not God can use his power if asked by them in prayer.

Many believe that God does intervene to change the course of history and can be seen like a superman who can turn back the clock, hold back the tide, divert hurricanes away from centres of population and so on.

Omnipresence

If God can do anything and knows everything then it is logical that he is *omnipresent* – that is, he can be everywhere at once. For Catholics, God is everywhere, mysteriously and mystically. This is an article of faith; it is not a matter of fact or certainty. The biggest problem facing Catholics is when adherents (believers) claim certainty. Only God can know things for sure, according to Catholic belief.

God and Catholics

Most Catholics come to know God through the second person of the **Trinity**, Jesus. Some find it hard to pray directly to God and choose to ask for help from **Mary** or one of the saints – this is called intercession. There are many examples of God talking directly to believers. This is known as a religious experience, or 'theophany', literally, a manifestation or appearance of God.

FOR INTEREST

The Universe, according to scientists, extends into infinite space. No one will ever get to the end of it. This means, for Catholics, that if they believe that God created the Universe he is either infinite himself or exists outside the physical universe. The technical word for this is 'metaphysical'.

FOR DEBATE

Discuss this very old theological 'chestnut': Could God create two hills without a valley between?

AO2 skills ACTIVITIES

Explore the reasons people use to support their belief or disbelief in God. Draw up a table and compare them with your work partner. Add to your own list any new ideas.

St Augustine wrote that human beings will always be restless until they learn to rest in God. It suggests that long-lasting happiness and contentment is impossible in this world. Examine the reasons why you agree or disagree with this teaching.

Jesus

The next two pages will help you to:

- explore the second person of the Trinity, Jesus
- explain Catholic beliefs about Jesus
- assess your own approach to the divinity of Jesus.

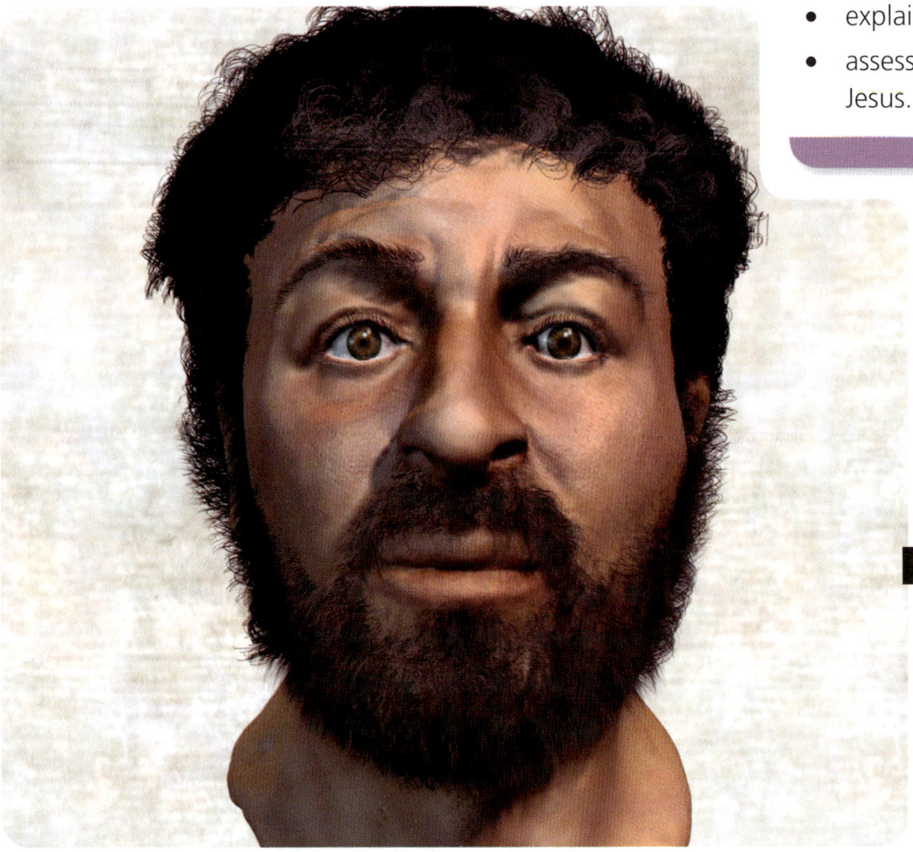

A modern photofit of Jesus of Nazareth.

The facts about Jesus

Jesus was a human being, aspects of whose life are known to history through the writings of ancient historians such as Tacitus (a Roman) and Josephus (a Jew). Jesus was born about 2000 years ago, he came from Nazareth in Galilee and was executed by the Romans for treason in Jerusalem. He was a preacher. **Catholics**, like all **Christians**, also believe that Jesus was God. Here are some other beliefs they hold about him:

- his was the **Virgin Birth** – he was born to **Mary**, who was miraculously still a virgin after he was conceived
- God becoming human is known as the **incarnation** – being 'made flesh'
- Jesus was related to John the Baptist
- he gave his most trusted **apostles** a foresight of **Heaven** at the Transfiguration
- Jesus rose from the dead, three days after he was executed by the Romans
- after his resurrection, Jesus ascended into Heaven; his body did not rot and wither in a grave.

AO1 skills ACTIVITIES

Rescue stories are popular in newspapers. Christians believe that Jesus came to rescue them from sin. Write a headline and accompanying article outlining how and why Jesus saved people.

The titles of Jesus

In the **gospels**, Jesus has a number of names and titles:

- Son of David, referring to his ancestral origins
- Son of Man, referring to the claims many made that he was the Messiah the people had been expecting
- King of the Jews, referring to the claims that his followers made of him
- Son of God, referring to the belief in Jesus' divinity that many followers instantly developed
- Holy One of God – this title is mostly used by evil spirits that Jesus was casting out of sick or diseased persons.

Jesus: God and man

Down through the centuries there have been debates over the relationship between Jesus' divinity and his humanity. The orthodox Catholic position is that Jesus was fully human and fully divine – he had both natures. This is another example of a matter of faith, not fact. It is hard to understand this and even harder to describe, so the best way to look at it is to see Jesus as God's representative on Earth.

Matthew 17:1–6

Six days later, Jesus took with him Peter and James and his brother John and led them up a high mountain by themselves. There in their presence he was transfigured: his face shone like the sun and his clothes became as dazzling as light. And suddenly Moses and Elijah appeared to them; they were talking with him. Then Peter spoke to Jesus. 'Lord,' he said, 'it is wonderful for us to be here; if you want me to, I will make three shelters here, one for you, one for Moses and one for Elijah.' He was still speaking when suddenly a bright cloud covered them with shadow, and suddenly from the cloud there came a voice which said, 'This is my Son, the Beloved; he enjoys my favour. Listen to him.'

AO2 skills ACTIVITIES

Catholics believe 'For our sake he (Jesus) was crucified under Pontius Pilate, he suffered death and was buried.' In pairs examine the times Jesus suffered emotionally and physically. Compare them to the ways in which people suffer today. What conclusions could you make?

Did Jesus really have to die to atone for people's sins (to have their sins forgiven)? Consider the answers a Catholic might give to these questions. Look up John 3:16–17 if you need help and then script a conversation between two friends discussing this question.

REMEMBER THIS

The **resurrection** is the most important doctrine for Catholics. Nothing else makes sense without it. By rising from the dead Jesus overcame the power of evil that had been put on the human race. This event puts Jesus at the mid-point of history. All good people who came before him were rescued from eternal suffering in Hell and all people who come after him have the chance to go to Heaven.

The Transfiguration (1594–5) by Ludovico Carracci.

The Holy Spirit

The next two pages will help you to:

- explore Catholic beliefs about the third person of the Trinity, the Holy Spirit
- explain Catholic beliefs about the Holy Spirit
- assess your own approach to the existence of the Holy Spirit.

Pope John Paul II releasing a dove from the Vatican as a sign of peace.

AO1 skills ACTIVITIES

The Holy Spirit has often been described as 'the love of God in action'. What do you think this means? Create a new symbol for the Holy Spirit that demonstrates this love and explain your choice.

The breath of God

A powerful way of understanding the **Holy Spirit** is as the 'breath of God'. This is because the breath of a person is only seen by the effect it has. Humans cannot see the wind, but they can see the effect it has as it ruffles the leaves on trees. A gentle breeze can be just as influential as a howling wind. A strong wind can be a positive force in nature, blowing away unwanted debris. It can also have devastating effects, like the hurricane that destroyed New Orleans, USA, in 2006.

In the **Old Testament** story of Elijah, the spirit of God is described as a 'still small voice' blowing gently into his ear and soothing his troubled mind. **Catholics** believe that when **Jesus** 'breathed his last' on the cross, the Holy Spirit continued God's work on Earth.

The Holy Spirit as a messenger

Catholicism developed out of Judaism, which, at the time of Jesus, had a very clear cosmology (study of the Universe). Early Catholics saw the Holy Spirit as a messenger from God passing between **Heaven** and Earth.

To symbolise this, the Holy Spirit is often portrayed as a dove. In the story of Noah, it is a dove that symbolically returns from dry land bearing the news that the deluge is over. For **Christians**, the dove has become a dual symbol of peace and the Holy Spirit.

The paraclete

In the writings of St John the Evangelist, the word *paraclete* (meaning 'advocate' or 'comforter') is used to show that the Holy Spirit did some of Jesus' work on his behalf. Jesus is seen as the advocate of his people and in his absence, after his death, the Holy Spirit works on his behalf. In other words, the Holy Spirit asks questions of God about his people and takes messages and prayers to him. In this sense the Holy Spirit is equal with Jesus. That is how the Holy Spirit is able to take up the third place in the **Trinity**. Catholics differ from some other parts of the Christian faith in their understanding of the relationships that Jesus and the Holy Spirit have with God the **Father**. Catholics believe that the Holy Spirit comes from Jesus as much as it comes from God.

Acts 2:1–4

When Pentecost day came round, they had all met together, when suddenly there came from heaven a sound as of a violent wind which filled the entire house in which they were sitting; and there appeared to them tongues as of fire; these separated and came to rest on the head of each of them. They were all filled with the Holy Spirit and began to speak different languages as the Spirit gave them power to express themselves.

MUST THINK ABOUT!

Many people, if asked, will acknowledge their belief in a spiritual realm – a place inhabited by good spirits (angels) and bad spirits (demons). If you believe that there may be spirits, it is quite likely that you will interpret paranormal or supernatural experiences as if a spirit had started to make itself known to you. If you are sceptical about a spiritual world, you may well interpret the same event as a trick of the mind, a psychological event or wind blowing through a door you left open.

AO2 skills ACTIVITIES

In the **gospel** accounts, Jesus was tempted by the devil while in the wilderness. Examine the evidence for the belief in a spiritual realm beyond this world.

The festival of Pentecost is often overlooked and under-celebrated in the Church's year. Create a publicity campaign that would raise the profile of Pentecost to equal that of Christmas and Easter. How do you think people might respond to this idea?

Frameworks for living

The next two pages will help you to:

- identify and understand the core teachings of Christianity
- explain how the core teachings help Christians to make decisions about how they should live
- consider your own views about the relevance of these core teachings to life today.

How do we know how we should live?

When Gordon Brown made a speech in May 2007 announcing that he wanted to lead the Labour Party and become Prime Minister, he spoke of his vision for Britain and of the influence that his parents had on him (his father was a Church of Scotland minister). He said, 'For me, my parents were – and their inspiration still is – my moral compass. The compass has guided me through each stage of my life. They taught me the importance of integrity and decency, treating people fairly – and duty to others...'

AO1 skills ACTIVITIES

What is a compass for? What do you think Gordon Brown means by a 'moral compass'? Who, or what, is your moral compass? Why is this? How do you decide what is right and wrong?

What gives Christians guidance for living?

The Ten Commandments

The Ten Commandments are one of the oldest sets of principles for living. They are over 3000 years old. Jews and **Christians** believe that they were given to Moses by God and were written on stone tablets. They provide clear guidance on how God expects people to behave. You can find the Commandments in Exodus 20:1–17 and the story of how God gave them to Moses in Exodus 19.

The Ten Commandments are part of the Torah, the Jewish scriptures. As a Jew, **Jesus** would have understood that the law was the revelation of God's will for how his people were to live. He would have been brought up to follow the Ten Commandments and he referred to them in his teaching. They describe a person's responsibility to God and their responsibility to others and can be divided into religious commandments, about the way people should behave towards God, and social commandments, about how people should treat each other.

Religious commandments

1. You shall have no other gods to rival me.
2. You shall not make yourself a carved image (to worship).
3. You shall not misuse the name of God.
4. Remember the Sabbath day and keep it holy.

Social commandments

5. Honour your father and your mother.
6. You shall not commit murder.
7. You shall not commit adultery.
8. You shall not steal.
9. You shall not give false evidence.
10. You shall not envy something which belongs to someone else.

AO1 skills ACTIVITIES

Read Mark 12:28–34, which asks that we love God and love others as much as we love ourselves. How easy is it to put this into practice in today's world? What would the problems be? How would the world be different if everybody tried to put this into practice?

The two great commandments

The **gospels** give a number of examples where people who were very knowledgeable about the Jewish law, and skilled in its interpretation, posed difficult questions for Jesus to answer. In Mark 12:28–34 you can read of one such incident when a teacher of the law asked Jesus this question: 'which is the first of all the commandments?' In his response Jesus chose the Shema, the Jewish declaration of faith found in Deuteronomy 6:4–5: 'Listen, Israel: Yahweh our God is the one, the only Yahweh. You must love Yahweh your God with all your heart, with all your soul, with all your strength.'

Jesus continued, 'The second is this: "Love your neighbour as yourself"', adding another commandment from Leviticus 19:18. The teacher of the law agreed with Jesus. This conversation shows that Jesus considered the Jewish scriptures to be the basis for the 'new commandments'.

Moses carried the two stone tablets on which were written the Ten Commandments down from the top of Mount Sinai. This picture is from a Victorian postcard.

The Sermon on the Mount

The Sermon on the Mount is a collection of blessings, parables, interpretations of the Torah and teachings about religious practices. Some of the core teachings of Christianity are found in these three chapters of Matthew. It is unlikely that Jesus taught all of these ideas at the same time but when the author of the gospel was compiling his story, he decided to put all these teachings of Jesus together.

Matthew's gospel was written for Jewish Christians and, just as Moses went to the top of Mount Sinai to receive the Torah from God, the author decided that he would have Jesus climb a mountain to teach his disciples, and the huge crowds who followed him, about these new principles for living. These teachings are sometimes called 'the new law'. They were given the title 'The Sermon on the Mount' and are found in Matthew 5–7.

AO1 skills ACTIVITIES

Compare the teachings of the Beatitudes (Matthew 5:1–12) with those of the Ten Commandments. What similarities and differences can you find between them?

The problem of evil

The next two pages will help you to:

- explore Catholic approaches to the problem of evil
- explain why Catholic teaching on forgiveness is challenging for some people
- evaluate your own views on suffering, death and forgiveness.

There are many incidents of natural evil in the world, such as this earthquake in China.

What's the problem?

Put simply, the problem of evil is a conundrum or puzzle.

- There is evil in the world.
- If God made everything, he must be responsible for the presence of evil in the world.
- If God is good why did he make evil?
- God knows everything, so if he knows something bad is going to happen, why does he not prevent it?

The conundrum can be answered like this.

- God is believed to be so loving that he gave his creation the free will to choose between good and evil.
- If humans have free will and can choose between good and evil, it is not surprising that sometimes they choose evil.

Most scholars accept that there are two types of evil:

- natural evil: events such as floods, hurricanes, droughts, earthquakes, landslides, tornadoes, tsunamis, etc.
- moral evil: actions such as wars, violence, crime, neglect, abuse, homelessness, etc.

AO1 skills ACTIVITIES

Create a collage using words and images to highlight natural and moral evil or problems in the world today. Make a suitable caption for your collage and discuss it with your work partner. Display the work for further consideration.

MUST THINK ABOUT!

Look at the two lists of different types of evil. Where would you put illness? The suffering and pain of sickness can be most people's experience of evil in the world. It is very hard to see any good in the death of a young person whose life is taken by cancer. Such an event will 'test the faith' of even the most devout of believers.

Catholic responses to evil

There are three broad types of response by **Catholics** to the presence of evil in the world.

Type	Examples	Catholic behaviours
Literal	Some Catholics believe that the devil exists in a real form and 'meddles' in human affairs to spread malice and vice throughout the world. They believe that people like Hitler are possessed by demons and need to be exorcised by a priest in order to be free to love once more.	Catholics who believe this will: • avoid temptation • go to confession to 'atone' for their sins • pray that good will conquer evil and that Jesus will redeem the world from its sinfulness.
Fatalistic	Other Catholics believe that God has given the world pain, suffering and sickness as a trial or test of faith. They see suffering as inevitable and that the task of Catholics is to accommodate this in their life and work every day to keep a balance of good things to offset the bad.	Catholics who believe this may: • undertake good works • visit the sick, needy or imprisoned • pray for fair treatment when the time comes to enter Heaven.
Rational	Most contemporary Catholics take the view that there is a purpose to pain, suffering and disease in the world, however hard it might be to understand this. Some go so far as to say that natural disasters are a wake-up call to the human community.	Catholics who believe this may: • pray for the courage to contribute usefully to the human community • give some of their time, money and effort to charitable causes • avoid making judgements about other people and their lifestyles.

Forgiveness of sins

One of the outstanding features of Christianity is its belief in and practice of forgiveness. The **Church** teaches that there is no **sin** a person can commit that is too grave for God to forgive. This is hard for ordinary people to understand as some sins or crimes appear unforgivable. It is important to remember, however, that there is nothing that God cannot do, so if he chooses to forgive – just like the father in the story of the Prodigal Son (Luke 15) – he can. The Sacrament of Reconciliation is the ceremony where this takes place officially (see Topic 4.6).

AO2 skills **ACTIVITIES**

Evil and suffering cause problems for those who believe in God. Explore the reasons for this and consider what the Christian response should be to the existence of evil in the world. Script a conversation between two people, one an atheist (a person who doesn't believe in God) and the other a Christian, which highlights the strengths and weaknesses of believing in a God in the face of evil.

Examine the relationship between suffering and evil. Discuss in small groups whether or not it is always necessary for suffering to follow from an evil deed. Amend your written response in the light of the points made by others.

The Last Things

The next two pages will help you to:

- explore Catholic approaches to the Last Things – the afterlife
- evaluate your own views on Heaven, Hell and Judgement.

Part of the 'Last Judgement' by Fra Angelico.

AO1 skills ACTIVITIES

Ask several class members what they believe about the afterlife. Write up their responses and draw your own conclusions. Create a symbol or picture of your view of life after death. Give reasons for your choice.

The afterlife

There are cases of people who have died (medical science suggested that their body had ceased all vital signs of life), who are reported to have 'come back from the dead'. These are called 'near-death experiences'. When they are recovered enough from the ordeal, the person concerned talks about what happened clearly. They tell of an experience of light drawing them in, and of white-robed beings that resemble humans.

It is important to remember that the reports of these experiences are as impossible to corroborate as miracles (see Topic 3.9) and visions (see Topic 2.7) are. They are, however, very real to the people who make them. For **Catholics**, the nature of what happens after the end of life is not as important as believing that there is an afterlife in the first place. The origins of Catholic approaches to the afterlife are found in **Jesus'** own teaching.

Judgement

Jesus left a clear statement of what will happen at the end of a person's life:

Matthew 25:31a, 33–35

When the Son of Man comes in his glory... He will place the sheep on his right hand and the goats on his left. Then the King will say to those on his right hand, 'Come, you whom my Father has blessed, take as your heritage the kingdom prepared for you since the foundation of the world. For I was hungry and you gave me food, I was thirsty and you gave me drink, I was a stranger and you made me welcome, lacking clothes and you clothed me, sick and you visited me, in prison and you came to see me.'

Heaven

According to Matthew, a person who has been engaged in acts of charity will go to **Heaven**. This is the Catholic view that also sees personal salvation as the goal of Catholics, something that can only be achieved by these good works. For Lutherans (see Topic 3.5), it is faith alone that will get a person into Heaven, and only then if they have been baptised.

Purgatory

Catholics also believe in **Purgatory**. Some people reach death unready for the fullness of life with God. The process of purifying them is known as Purgatory. This belief explains why Catholics pray for the dead rather than just remembering them.

Hell

The traditional notion of **Hell** was of a place of eternal fire, pain and anguish. If you shut your eyes and think of the word it often conjures up images of heat or flames and ghoulish demons carrying pitchforks, with red as the background colour.

Hell is really the absence of God for all eternity. It might be better imagined as a place of deep cold – maybe even the icy wastes of an arctic desert – a barren wilderness, bleak and stark. It is God who puts the warmth into the Universe and whose absence would be chilling. To be cut off forever from the communion of the saints would be unbearable for Catholics.

MUST THINK ABOUT!

Can a person who has led a good life and has been committed to acts of charity, but who has never gone to **church** or shown any commitment to Jesus, still go to Heaven?

It has to be assumed that Heaven will be, for those who get there, an eternal banquet. This idea comes from Jesus and is repeated frequently through this book.

AO2 skills ACTIVITIES

St Paul wrote in 1 Corinthians 15:55b 'Death, where is your sting?' Examine the meaning behind these words and explore whether or not you think they would provide consolation for mourners and the grieving.

It has been said that people live their lives according to how they understand their death. Consider the meaning of this statement and explore the differences between the life of a Catholic and the life of an atheist. You may wish to refer to Psalm 23 (Psalm 22 in the Vulgate).

Mary and the Communion of Saints

The next two pages will help you to:

- explore the role of Mary and her significance to Catholics
- explore the Catholic concept of sainthood and its significance
- examine the lives of particular saints and give reasons why Catholics consider them important.

'The Madonna and Child' by Sassoferrato.

AO1 skills ACTIVITIES

Read John 19:25–27. Describe the relationship between Mary and Jesus and give your reasons. Explain how this text might be used to help build up family relationships.

Mary, the Mother of God

Catholics pray at Mass, saying 'Holy Mary, Mother of God…' This presents a real challenge of faith for the following reasons:

- If God created everything, how can he have created his own mother?
- How could any human being create God?
- Does this means that **Mary** should be considered as co-equal to **Jesus** and the **Holy Spirit**?

Many **Christian** denominations reject these possibilities and see Mary as a remarkable woman but not the Mother of God. In order to understand this you need to understand the **Trinity** first (see Topic 1.2). Once it is accepted that Jesus and God are co-equal, it begins to make sense that Mary, who was the birth Mother of Jesus, can also be the mother of God in human form.

Mary as a model

There are many things that Catholics admire about Mary. First, she accepted the will of God into her life. The likelihood is that she was about 14 when the angel Gabriel visited her and told her that she was to be the mother of Jesus. Second, she witnessed the dreadful tragedy that befell her **son** on the cross. Mary is said to have held Jesus in her arms when his body was taken down from the cross. Third, Mary became the hub of the early community that developed in the aftermath of Jesus' death, despite her sorrow and loss. Catholics believe that for each of these reasons, Mary is deserving of their utmost respect, admiration and, in some cases, devotion.

The devotional prayer to Mary that is said every Sunday at Mass

Hail Mary, full of grace,
The Lord is with thee,
Blessed art though among women,
and blessed is the fruit of thy womb, Jesus.
Holy Mary, Mother of God,
Pray for us sinners, now, and at the hour of our death.
Amen

The Communion of Saints

Mary was recognised very early as a saint of the Church. In devotional pictures which feature her, she is represented wearing a halo. Other pictures also use the halo to indicate saints. Many of these people were made saints through the process of beatification and canonisation.

There are thousands of others who have become saints, all of whom form the Communion of Saints. The Communion of Saints is a belief, not a fact. It is Catholicism's attempt to explain how all these people whose earthly life has ended are in **Heaven**, constantly asking God to be merciful to human beings and allow them to enter into the Kingdom of Heaven. For Catholics the purpose of the Communion of Saints is to intercede (plead) on their behalf. If you visit ancient cathedrals or larger churches, you will see the Communion of Saints portrayed like a jury in stained-glass windows or sculptures.

The word 'communion' creates an image that is quite deliberate. Holy Communion takes place in the Mass, which is supposed to represent the Messianic Banquet as foretold in the scriptures. Being in communion with the saints suggests the participation of ordinary folk in the afterlife.

FOR DEBATE

Many Protestant thinkers and writers have criticised the Catholic practice of praying for and to the dead, including saints. They believe that people should talk directly to God by making their own prayers. As a class, debate the question: 'Do you think it is more effective to talk directly to God, or does it help to have people through whom the messages can be communicated?' Take a poll of opinions and write the responses up as a class statement on the issue.

AO2 skills ACTIVITIES

Catholics regard the Virgin Mary not only as a model of the Christian life but as an essential part of Christian worship. Defend this position to a friend who believes that Mary was an admirable woman but not worthy of special devotion.

Assess the effect of believing that the saints are supporting you in your faith and cheering you on.

Saints

The next two pages will help you to:

- identify and understand what Christians mean by saints
- explain why particular people are regarded as saints
- reflect on what might cause someone to live a life which is considered saintly.

Saints

The **New Testament** uses the word 'saint' to describe members of the early **Christian Church**. Soon, however, the word was used for people who were especially devoted to their religion or lived a particular life of Christian love. The process by which a person becomes a saint is called 'canonisation'. The first person to be canonised by the Pope was Bishop Udalric of Augsburg, in 993 CE.

Since the 12th century, the Pope has also 'beatified' particularly holy people after their death. The person is then called 'Blessed'. Beatification may be followed by canonisation but usually not until 50 years after the person's death and when it is established that they have performed at least two miracles since their death.

The Vatican Congregation for the Causes of Saints investigates cases of sainthood and the final decision is then made by the Pope. It is worth remembering that when considering a person for sainthood, the first thing which the congregation does is to appoint someone who has to try to prove that the person was not a saint

AO1 skills ACTIVITIES

What do you think are the characteristics of a saint? Discuss with a partner what it is that particularly makes someone a saint.

Maximilian Kolbe

Maximilian Kolbe was a Polish monk, born in 1894. In 1907 he and his elder brother Francis joined a Franciscan seminary at Lwów, and he took his final vows in Rome in 1914 when he was just 20 years old. He became a priest four years later and founded a monastery near Warsaw and another one on the outskirts of Nagasaki in Japan.

During the Second World War, Maximilian provided shelter to refugees, hiding 2000 Jews in his friary. He was arrested by the Gestapo on 17 February 1941 and was later imprisoned in the infamous Auschwitz prison camp.

In July 1941, following the disappearance of a man from the hut in which Kolbe lived, ten other inmates were ordered to be starved to death. One of them was so distressed that Maximilian offered to take his place. After three weeks only four were still alive. Maximilian was then killed by an injection of carbolic acid.

Maximilian was canonised in 1982 by John Paul II, who called him 'The Patron Saint of Our Difficult Century'. He is also the patron saint of drug addicts, political prisoners, families, journalists and the pro-life movement.

Blessed Mother Teresa

Mother Teresa of Calcutta was born Agnes Gonxha Bojaxhiu in 1910, in Albania. She became a nun in Ireland at the age of 18, and then went to Darjeeling, in India, when she was 27.

While she was principal of a **Catholic** high school in Calcutta, she became distressed by the number of sick and dying people on the streets of the city. In 1948 she was given permission to leave the school and begin a ministry among the sick.

In 1950 the Missionaries of Charity led by Mother Teresa was approved within the archdiocese of Calcutta. Later the order became a pontifical congregation under the direct jurisdiction of Rome. The members of the congregation take four vows: as well as the vows of poverty, chastity and obedience, the fourth vow pledges service to the poor. Mother Teresa believed that the poor were the embodiment of **Christ**.

The Nirmal Hriday (Pure Heart) Home for Dying Destitutes in Calcutta was opened in 1952. Mother Teresa was awarded the Nobel Peace Prize in 1979. She resigned from the Missionaries of Charity in March 1997 because of poor health and died six months later.

She was beatified by Pope John Paul II in October 2003.

Saint Pio of Pietrelcina (Padre Pio).

Padre Pio

Padre Pio was born Francesco Forgione in 1887 in the south of Italy. As a youth he claimed to have experienced heavenly visions. He joined a friary at Morcone in 1903 and was ordained as a priest in Benevento in 1910. In 1916, he was moved to an agricultural community, Our Lady of Grace Capuchin Friary, in San Giovanni Rotondo. He stayed at the friary until his death.

Padre Pio suffered from poor health all his life and nothing appeared to help his conditions.

He is best remembered because he bore the stigmata, visible signs in his body of the wounds of **Jesus** at the crucifixion. By 1919 he was becoming famous and many Catholics regarded him as a symbol of hope after the First World War (1914–1918). He is famous for the quote, 'Pray, hope and don't worry'.

Although some people claimed his wounds were faked, in 1939 Pope Pius XII encouraged people to visit Padre Pio, and in the 1960s Pope Paul VI dismissed all the charges made against him.

Padre Pio died in 1968 and more than 100,000 people attended the funeral. The miraculous cure of an Italian after asking for the prayers of Padre Pio was accepted as a miracle and in 1999 John Paul II declared him blessed. After a further miracle he was canonised in 2005.

AO2 skills **ACTIVITIES**

'Saints are just ordinary people who care for others; there is nothing else special about them.' Discuss this statement and consider other views.

Catholic Church

The next two pages will help you to:

- explain what is meant by the Catholic Church
- describe the characteristics of the Catholic Church
- present an argument outlining your approach to the authority of the Church.

The Council of Constantinople 381 CE was held at the Hagia Irene church.

The origins of the Catholic Church

Some people say they have **catholic** tastes. Usually this means that they like a broad range of music, food, drinks and literature, or other items that are matters of personal preference. This is an appropriate use of the word 'catholic', which means 'universal'.

When the Nicene **Creed** was formulated and finally published in 381 CE, at the Council of Constantinople, the **Church** covered the whole of the known Western world. This is because it had become the adopted religion of the Roman Empire, which stretched across the whole of Europe and into North Africa and Western Asia. The Americas were not known to the Romans, nor were most of Africa, Asia and the Pacific region.

What is the Church?

It is important to understand the meaning of the original word for 'church'. The Greeks called it *ekklesia*, which means 'assembly', often expressed as 'the people of God'. The Church included everyone who believed that God had called them to be a member. Today there are many organisations that describe themselves as a Church, all of whom are denominations of Christianity. The largest denomination is the Roman Catholic Church, which has over 1 billion members, and is headed by the Pope, based in the Vatican, Rome.

As you will see in Topic 4, the word 'church' is also used to refer to places of worship.

AO1 skills ACTIVITIES

Make a list of all the groups you belong to inside and outside of school. Create a chart or diagram to show how much time you spend in these groups in one week. Describe how and explain why human beings seem to like belonging to a group.

The Magisterium of the Church

The body that decides who is in or out of the Catholic Church is the Sacred Congregation for the Doctrine of the Faith. This is the group of people who decide on matters of faith and morals and who set out the formal teachings of the Church in documents (see Topic 6). The Church is governed by senior priests, usually in the role of cardinal or bishop. These people form what is known as the teaching authority of the Church, or the 'Magisterium'. A committee of the Magisterium published the Catechism of the Church in 1993, which determines what is taught in parishes and in Catholic schools. Those who stray from its messages are regarded as heretics. You can read this important document online at the Vatican website.

Paragraph 811 of the Catechism of the Catholic Church

'This is the sole Church of Christ, which in the Creed we profess to be one, holy, catholic and apostolic.' These four characteristics, inseparably linked with each other, indicate essential features of the Church and her mission. The Church does not possess them of herself; it is Christ who, through the Holy Spirit, makes his Church one, holy, catholic, and apostolic, and it is he who calls her to realise each of these qualities.

The organisation and authority of the Church

Read the extract from the Catechism. Look at the four characteristics that are described. Notice how the Church requires its members to acknowledge the role that the **apostles** played in its development. Notice also that this is a challenge to anyone setting up a Church – it can only be seen as authoritative if it has links right back to the early community in Jerusalem. Through apostolic succession from St Peter, the Catholic Church believes it is the authentic voice of **Jesus** in the world today. Whilst power is effectively held by the College of Cardinals, in the mind of most Catholics, it is the Pope who has overall control over what the Church says and does.

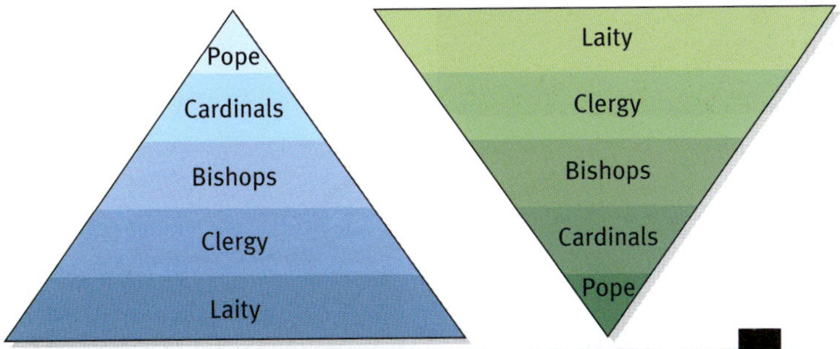

On the left is the traditional model of the Church in its hierarchical form. On the right is a model of the Church based on the idea of the service of the people of God.

FOR INTEREST

Did you know that every cardinal – there are about 200 in the world – as well as being the bishop of a diocese also has to have a parish in Rome. The Cardinal Archbishop of England has the Church of Santa Maria Sopra Minerva, which is right opposite the Pantheon, a building that has stood in Rome for hundreds of years and was a shrine for the early pagan religions that characterised the Roman Empire.

AO2 skills ACTIVITIES

Demonstrate, as if in a court of law, the authority and importance of the Church in society today. Put together a case which could be presented to the rest of the class.

The Church is a worldwide organisation. Explore the strengths and weaknesses of belonging to such a large group of people who come from different countries and speak various languages, yet all believe in the same God.

The effect and importance of beliefs for Catholics

The next two pages will help you to:

- examine the effect of some key beliefs on Catholics
- explore how and in what ways they are important for the faith
- assess the value of Catholic teaching, beliefs and practice in people's lives.

St Peter being led to his execution in Rome.

A case study approach

One of the best ways of examining the effects of beliefs on practice and customs is through case studies. This way someone can understand from a narrative what it actually feels like for a real person.

In the case studies that follow, the gender, identity and location of each character is fictional, but the events are real and actually happened. You may be able to add your own stories which either support or contradict those here. Some of them may appear a little extreme but it needs to be remembered that, in some parts of the world, being religious can be risky. People still die for what they believe.

AO1 skills ACTIVITIES

On five separate sticky notes or cards write down a familiar aspect of life, for example relationships, employment or problems. Allow a class member to choose one topic and ask them to describe and explain the teachings given by the Bible or the Church about this subject.

Case study 1

A young woman who had been a Christian all her life and had attended Sunday worship in her home church suddenly began to take seriously the practices of one of her very good friends. This person, a Catholic, was convinced that her personal salvation depended on carrying out charitable works. Every year she would pay from her own purse, to travel to the Holy Land on a diocesan pilgrimage to assist with moving the elderly from hotel to hotel and from sacred site to sacred site.

Although she had been brought up in her own tradition to believe that faith alone was enough to get to Heaven, the woman decided that she wanted to become a Catholic and to earn her place in Heaven by undertaking good works herself.

Case study 2

Returning home from school one day, a 15-year-old African boy found soldiers inside the house, beating his father. He was quickly arrested and taken away. Whilst being tortured he was asked to deny his faith in God and in the Catholic Church. His guards promised to let him go if he would give up his beliefs. He refused and was eventually clubbed to death.

Case study 3

A Catholic teacher in a Southern state of America was appalled to find that the principal of his school was insisting that the Creationist approach to the origins of the Universe be taught in science lessons. The teacher was not able to reconcile his firmly held religious beliefs and rational scientific approach to the curriculum with this illogical, inconsistent and prejudicial new way of teaching. He resigned.

Case study 4

Visiting a local Mosque with a group from her local youth club, a Catholic teenager was struck by the name of Mary, the Mother of Jesus, written on the walls of the office of the Imam. She asked why this was and had it explained that Mary was a perfect example of a Muslim, because she had submitted her life to the will of Allah. This experience had a profound effect on the girl, who was inspired to do two things: She renewed her own devotion to Our Lady and committed to pray the rosary once a week. She also established an inter-faith youth club between her church and the Muslim community in her town. She arranged talks so the groups could get to know each other better and social events aimed at bonding the two communities. She became a local heroine.

REMEMBER THIS

In the early Church, when persecution was common, the sin of 'apostasy' was created. Apostasy means to deny your faith under pressure. It is what St Peter is accused of when he denied even knowing Jesus on the night of the Passover in Jerusalem.

AO2 skills ACTIVITIES

Brainstorm the words 'morality' and 'religion' with your work partner. Compare and contrast the results. Role-play a conversation between two friends: one who believes that all good and kind people should go to heaven and one who thinks that religious beliefs and practice are also needed for salvation.

GradeStudio

Welcome to the Grade Studio

GCSE is about what you can do, not what you can't do. You need to know what examiners want in your answers so that you can get the best possible marks. In GCSE Religious Studies there are two things that examiners are looking for. These are called assessment objectives (AO). Questions are designed to help examiners find out how well you do in each assessment objective.

Graded examples for this topic

AO1

AO1 questions test what you know and how well you can explain and analyse things. Let's look at some AO1 questions to see what examiners are expecting you to do.

Question

Explain why the Creeds are important to some Roman Catholics. **[6 marks]**

Possible steps to answer the question: What should an answer be like and how do examiners work out what is a good or a poor response?

Examiners use levels to measure the responses. There are three levels for AO1. A good answer will not only give a definition, it will explain in some detail what it means, how it links to other beliefs and how it affects a Christian's life. You could build an answer like this:

Student's answer

Catholics always say the Creed towards the beginning of the Mass.

Examiner's comment

The answer is accurate but it lacks any additional information, such as who it is said by and why it occurs at the beginning (Level 1).

Student's answer

Catholics always say the Creed together at the beginning of the Mass to remind themselves straightaway of their beliefs. By saying it together they show they are united and proud of their faith.

Examiner's comment

This is a satisfactory answer. It makes several important points: firstly, that that they say it together; secondly, that there is a reason for it being said at the beginning of the Mass; thirdly, that saying the Creed serves the purposes of reminding, uniting and declaring their faith to other people (Level 2).

Student's improved answer

Catholics say the Creeds because they date back to the time of the apostles and the early followers of Christ. They make clear to believers and non-believers what Christians believe in and can be helpful to refer to when there are misunderstandings. The Creeds became the basis for most of the later teachings of the Church and were used as a teaching aid for all Christians to show what is the truth. Like any agreed statement of belief, the Creeds help strengthen and unite Christians in their faith.

Examiner's comment

This is a good answer. It explains some of the history behind the Creeds. It makes clear how the Creeds are useful for believers and non-believers and how they can be used to combat heresy (Level 3).

AO2

The Ten Commandments are the only rules that Christians need. **[12 marks]**

AO2 questions are worth 50 per cent of the marks for each question, so you must practise expressing other people's views and develop your own view and support it with evidence.

You also need to practise holding back from expressing your own view until you have explained and made a comment about the views of others.

Often candidates lose marks because they focus too much on their own view, forgetting to express other views.

This limits what might otherwise be a good response to Level 1 or Level 2

Student's answer

The Ten Commandments are very important to Christians because they were given by God.

Examiner's comment

The answer gives important information about the Ten Commandments but does not really answer the question.

Student's answer

The Ten Commandments are very important to Christians because they were given by God. However, Jesus said that loving God and your neighbour were the two most important commandments.

Examiner's comment

This answer is satisfactory but now needs to give more detail and a supported personal view. (Level 2)

Student's improved answer

The Ten Commandments are very important to Christians because they were given to Moses by God when the Israelites were in the desert. However, Jesus said that loving God and your neighbour were the two most important commandments. He also said that he would not change the Law and that people should still follow the Ten Commandments. I think that the Ten Commandments are very important but Christians also need to follow the Two Commandments that Jesus gave as well as his other teachings in the Sermon on the Mount and the teachings of the Church.

Examiner's comment

This is a good answer. There are two points of view which are both supported as well as a well-supported personal viewpoint. (Level 4)

These specimen answers provide an outline of how you could construct your response. Space does not allow us to give a full response. The examiner will be looking for more detail in your actual exam responses.

Remember and Reflect

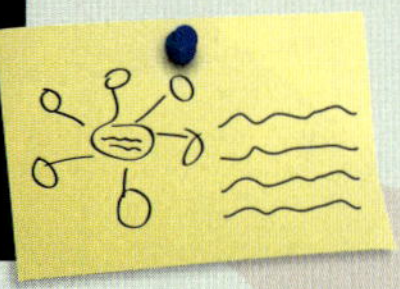

AO1 Describe, explain and analyse, using knowledge and understanding

	Find the answer on:
1 Name the three persons of God who are referred to as the Trinity.	PAGE 8
2 Name the prayer that Catholics say at Mass which sets out all their core beliefs.	PAGE 7
3 Why do Catholics believe that God made everything in the Universe?	PAGE 10–11
4 Approximately when did Jesus of Nazareth live?	PAGE 12
5 Explain why Catholics believe that Jesus was God in human form.	PAGE 13
6 Name three ways in which the Holy Spirit is described by Catholics.	PAGE 14–15
7 Explain how a person becomes a saint.	PAGE 24
8 How and in what ways does Mary the mother of Jesus hold a special place in the Catholic tradition?	PAGE 22–23
9 Describe how Catholics account for the existence of evil in the world.	PAGE 18–19
10 What do Catholics mean when they talk about the 'forgiveness of sins'?	PAGE 19
11 How do Catholics believe it is possible to achieve eternal life in Heaven?	PAGE 21
12 What do Catholics believe is the alternative to eternal life in Heaven?	PAGE 21
13 What effect is religious belief supposed to have on a Catholic's life?	PAGE 28–29
14 The Ten Commandments fall into two types. What are they? Give two examples of each type.	PAGE 16
15 What are the two great commandments?	PAGE 17

AO2 Use evidence and reasoned argument to express and evaluate personal responses, informed insights, and differing viewpoints

1 Do you believe that God created the Universe? Use the evidence from scientific enquiry to support your answer.

2 Catholics believe that it is possible for God to have designed everything, from the tiniest portion of DNA within a single cell to the individual strands of hair on a person's head (and there are about 6.7 billion people in the world). Do you think this is possible? Give reasons for your answer.

3 'Jesus, God and Man.' Do you think it is possible that God could have taken on human form and lived as a man? Give reasons for your answer.

4 Do you think supernatural events are 'interruptions' of the natural world by spirits, or do you think they are tricks of the mind or have rational explanations? Support your argument with evidence from the media or other sources.

5 It is likely that Mary was only about 14 years of age when she conceived Jesus. In the Jewish community in which she lived, pregnancy before marriage would have been considered a disgrace and would have brought shame on her family. What do you think gave Mary the courage to go through with the task of bringing Jesus into the world?

6 Is there a crime or a sin which a person could commit that God should not forgive? Write a full answer to this question, setting out the reasons for your opinion.

7 Why do you think it is common for religious people to believe in an afterlife? Answer this question with reference to Catholic teaching and to the religious ideas of other people whose beliefs you know.

Topic 2: Special days and pilgrimage

The Big Picture

In this Topic you will be examining:

- the main festivals of the Catholic Church
- the important feast days of the Catholic Church
- places of pilgrimage visited by Catholics
- the reasons why Catholics celebrate or make pilgrimages.

What?

You will:

- examine Sunday worship
- look at Easter, Christmas and other important festivals
- study some well-known places of pilgrimage in Catholicism
- explore the reasons for the festivals and the reasons why Catholics make pilgrimages.

Why?

Because:

- knowing the underlying reasons for festivals helps you to understand religious customs and practices
- understanding the symbolism of festivals helps you to understand the beliefs associated with them
- exploring the reasons why people make pilgrimages can help you to understand their motivation and inspiration
- evaluating the reasons for worship can help you to create a picture of the belief systems of a religion.

How?

By:

- looking at key ceremonies, ritual and symbols used during the festivals
- exploring the beliefs that underpin these events
- comparing and contrasting your own life experiences with these events in order to develop empathy.

Pope John Paul II blessing the crowds in St Peter's Square, Rome.

GET STARTED

Gather together as many versions of the Bible as you can. With the help of your teacher find the Christmas story. Notice anything? Go back and search again... Did you find anything new? Now answer these questions:

Is there any mention of turkeys, pine trees, tinsel, snow, fairies, mince pies or alcohol? Why do you think they have become important parts of the way that Christmas is celebrated?

Develop your knowledge

Special days and pilgrimages

Leonardo da Vinci's painting 'The Last Supper', which hangs in the Santa Maria della Grazie in Milan, Italy

KEY INFORMATION

- Catholics have a calendar of religious events known as the liturgical cycle. The events throughout the liturgical cycle are marked by different types of Mass and other celebrations. Many of the events are shared with other Christian denominations.
- The most important festival for Catholics is Easter, beginning with the three-day Triduum. Easter marks the crucifixion of Christ in Jerusalem. The Triduum starts with Holy (Maundy) Thursday, which commemorates the Last Supper that Christ shared with his apostles and ends on Holy Saturday.
- The period of Lent, leading up to Easter, is a period of fasting, when many Christians try to give something up as a mark of penitence.

KEY QUESTIONS

KNOWLEDGE AND UNDERSTANDING

How do Catholics celebrate the main events in the Christian calendar?

Why do Catholics sometimes expend considerable money and effort to go on pilgrimage?

ANALYSIS AND EVALUATION

What is to be gained by making a pilgrimage?

Why do Christians consider Easter to be more significant than Christmas?

How can visiting places that were important 2000 years ago be important today?

- Advent and Christmas are important festivals celebrating the birth (incarnation) of Jesus.
- Christians and Jews mark the Sabbath as a day of rest. For Christians, the Sabbath is on Sunday, while for Jews, the Sabbath is on Saturday.
- Many Catholics will make pilgrimages to sites of particular importance. These include sites from the life of Christ, such as Bethlehem (where Christ was born), Nazareth (where he lived) and Jerusalem, where he was executed. Other important sites include Rome, where the Basilica of St Peter is built over the site of St Peter's tomb, and Santiago di Compostela, in Spain, the site of St James's tomb.
- Pilgrimages are also made to places where there have been reports of visions of the Virgin Mary. The most famous of these is Lourdes, in France, and there are others in Mexico and Portugal.
- Saints are often commemorated at the places where they lived or died. Canterbury Cathedral is revered as the site of the assassination of St Thomas à Becket. Croagh Patrick is a mountain in Ireland where people will go to pray to St Patrick.
- The holy men and women of the Church are celebrated at special times in the year and sometimes in special places. Some of these special places are the sites of Christian communities where people can go for rest and retreat.

KEY WORDS

Advent The period beginning on the fourth Sunday before Christmas.

Ash Wednesday The first day of Lent. In some churches, penitents receive the sign of the Cross in ashes on their forehead.

Christmas The festival commemorating the birth of Christ (25 December).

crucifixion The Roman method of executing criminals and traitors by fastening them to a cross until they died. Used to execute Jesus Christ.

Easter The Christian festival to commemorate the resurrection of Christ from the dead.

festival A special occasion in the Church when an important event is celebrated.

Good Friday The Friday in Holy Week, commemorating the day when Christ was executed.

Holy (Maundy) Thursday The Thursday in Holy Week, commemorating the Last Supper.

Holy Week The week before Easter, when Christians recall the last week of Christ's life on Earth.

incarnation The doctrine that God took human form in Jesus Christ.

Lent The 40 days leading up to Easter.

liturgy The service of worship in a religious ceremony according to a prescribed ritual.

Mass A name for the Eucharist.

Palm Sunday The Sunday before Easter, commemorating the entry of Christ into Jerusalem.

paschal Anything to do with the Christian feast of Easter.

passion The sufferings of Jesus Christ, especially in the time leading up to his crucifixion.

Pentecost Fifty days after Easter, Catholics celebrate the birth of the Church as they commemorate the arrival of the Holy Spirit.

pilgrimage A journey to a special place usually associated with a religious event, person or particular type of worship.

Sabbath The day of rest.

Triduum The three important ceremonies of Easter: the Mandatum on Holy Thursday, the Good Friday liturgy and the Vigil Mass on Holy Saturday.

FOR INTEREST

In 1647, under the leadership of Oliver Cromwell, Parliament banned the celebration of Christmas in England. It was thought that Christmas celebrations were too heavily influenced by pagan traditions and symbols. Even using the word 'Christmas' was disapproved of as taking the Lord's name in vain. The ban was eventually lifted in 1660 (Cromwell died in 1658). Some denominations, such as Jehovah's Witnesses, still do not celebrate Christmas.

Liturgical calendar

The next two pages will help you to:

- understand the key parts of the liturgical cycle
- associate particular religious ceremonies with the relevant part of the liturgical cycle
- explain the reasons why Catholics celebrate when and how they do.

The circle of life

In every walk of life there are patterns. There are some people who will point to the birth of a baby as a new life when an elderly person has died. Each year people celebrate their own birthdays as a means of marking the passage of time. Seasons come and go: winter becomes spring and new life bursts out of hibernation; the summer settles in and eventually gives way to autumn as plants die away, the harvest is gathered and nature closes down again for winter.

The Church's cycle

The Church also has a cycle, known as the liturgical cycle (or sometimes called the liturgical year or calendar). The liturgical cycle begins with **Advent**, the four weeks leading up to **Christmas** (the birth or **incarnation** of Jesus Christ), and moves on into the new calendar year with the feast of the Epiphany. This is the time when the visit of the wise men – probably philosophers or mystics from the East – are said to have visited Jesus at his birthplace in Bethlehem.

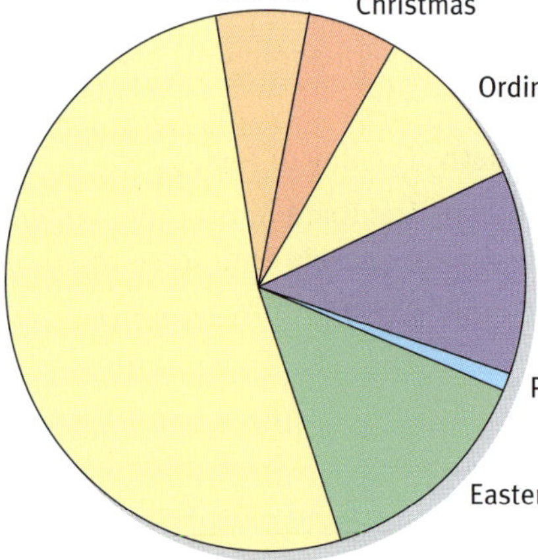

Ash Wednesday marks the start of the season of **Lent**. This is a 40-day period of fasting before **Easter**. The length of Lent was chosen to remember the 40 years Moses spent in the wilderness with the Israelites and the 40 days Jesus spent in the wilderness preparing for his life on Earth. Many Christians try to give up something for Lent.

Lent finishes on Holy Saturday, at the end of **Holy Week**, on the day before Easter Sunday. The last week of Lent overlaps with Holy Week, when the Church enters into the celebration of Easter,

AO1 skills ACTIVITIES

Make a list of all the special days you and your family celebrate every year. Draw a symbol for each. Choose five particular occasions and describe how and explain why you celebrate them.

REMEMBER THIS

All dates in the Christian calendar are approximate. For example, no one knows exactly when Jesus was born. Easter is more easily dated because it coincided with the Jewish festival of Passover. Passover is governed by the cycles of the moon, which shape the Jewish calendar. In Catholic terms Easter is therefore a 'movable feast'.

AO2 skills ACTIVITIES

The liturgical calendar reminds believers of the main events in the life of Jesus and the Church. Examine the advantages and disadvantages of following such a calendar.

commemorating when Jesus was **crucified** and rose from the dead. The Easter season, or Eastertide, is the period of 50 days from Easter Sunday to **Pentecost** Sunday or Whitsun. It is called Whitsun because white was traditionally worn on that Sunday. After Pentecost, the Church is entering summer (in the northern hemisphere) and a period known as the Ordinary time. The last Sunday of the liturgical year is marked with the **Festival** of Christ the King. This is the last Sunday before the start of Advent.

Some important feast days

In the past, Catholics were obliged to attend **Mass** on holy days throughout the year in addition to Easter Sunday and Christmas Day. Many feast days are now celebrated on the nearest Sunday in the UK but they were, until recently:

- the Feast of Saints Peter and Paul (29 June)
- the Ascension of Our Lord (40 days after the Resurrection)
- the Feast of Corpus Christi (Thursday after Pentecost)
- the Assumption of Our Lady (15 August)
- Epiphany (6 January), or Twelfth Night as it is known in Western Christianity
- All Saints Day (1 November).

Some branches of the Church also required attendance at Mass on 1 January to celebrate Mary as the Mother of God, 8 December to celebrate her Immaculate Conception and 19 March to celebrate the life of her husband Joseph. In some countries this is celebrated on 1 May as the feast of St Joseph the worker.

Other feasts in the calendar

Each saint of the Church has a feast day. These occur throughout the year and in the past many children were named after the saint on whose feast day they were born.

MUST THINK ABOUT!

If you are lucky enough to travel to the southern hemisphere or even to the tropics around December, you will be struck by the contrast between the heat of summer and the advertising of Christmas. Seeing Father Christmas in his sleigh with his reindeer is odd.

REMEMBER THIS

The seasons of the liturgical cycle are marked out by 'liturgical colours'. The vestments a priest wears, altar cloths and dressings, and the chalice veil are all changed. The normal colour is green. Red is used at Pentecost, symbolising the Holy Spirit. White is used at Easter to symbolise the resurrection, or at weddings to symbolise joy. Pink is used on Mothering Sunday, and purple during Lent to symbolise suffering.

AO1 skills ACTIVITIES

Most celebrations are fixed in the calendar and occur on the same date each year. What response would you give to a younger family member who thinks it is boring to do the same thing at the same time each year?

AO2 skills ACTIVITIES

Form a class circle. In turn, say one reason for and one against the notion that only believers should celebrate Christian festivals such as Christmas. Write up all the arguments you remember.

Festivals 1: Easter and the Triduum

The next two pages will help you to:

- distinguish the Easter ceremonies from other parts of the Christian calendar
- understand the beliefs that support Catholic rituals during the Easter Triduum
- evaluate Catholic liturgical practices and account for why they take place.

Holy Week

Holy Week starts on the Sunday before Easter Sunday, known as **Palm Sunday**. This day commemorates Christ's arrival in Jerusalem, and is named to remember the palm leaves laid in front of Christ as he rode into Jerusalem. In many churches, Palm Sunday is marked with palm leaves (often tied in the shape of a cross) being given out to the congregation.

AO1 skills ACTIVITIES

Make a list of at least ten key words to do with the Easter period. Make a word search for your work partner to fill in.

The Triduum

Holy Week culminates with the **Triduum**. The Triduum marks the three days from the evening of Holy Thursday to the evening of Easter Saturday, with special **Masses** taking place on each day. The word 'Triduum' comes from the Latin for 'three days'.

The Mandatum – Holy Thursday liturgy

On the night before he died, Jesus shared his last supper with the apostles, a meal that is commemorated in a special Mass called the 'Mandatum'. This is from the Latin word for 'command' and is used to remind Catholics of Jesus' instructions to the apostles to serve the community as he had. The day is often now called **Maundy Thursday**.

The Mandatum is a special Mass, because the priest, acting in the role of Jesus, washes the feet of twelve members of the congregation. In Jesus' time, this would have been a task carried out by the lowest member of the household, usually a slave. Jesus was demonstrating his teaching that every priest should be the servant to his community.

At the consecration, no bell is rung. Instead a loud crack is sounded to symbolise the breaking of Jesus' body and the horror about to happen.

After Mass the altar is stripped bare and the congregation are invited to stay and 'watch', repeating the acts of the apostles in the garden of Gethsemane, the night before Jesus died.

AO2 skills ACTIVITIES

Until recently school holidays were always fixed around the important Christian **festivals**. In 2008 the Easter weekend was celebrated before the renamed 'Spring holiday'. Examine the strengths and weaknesses for the celebration of Christianity of having these festivals separate from national holidays.

Matthew 26:36–38

Then Jesus came with them to a plot of land called Gethsemane; and he said to his disciples, 'Stay here while I go over there to pray.' He took Peter and the two sons of Zebedee with him. And he began to feel sadness and anguish. Then he said to them, 'My soul is sorrowful to the point of death. Wait here and stay awake with me.'

The Good Friday liturgy

Non-Christians often express their surprise that Catholics celebrate the death by **crucifixion** of their founder, and they may be confused that the day is named **Good Friday**. It is called Good Friday because Christians believe that it was good that Jesus died so that he could redeem the world from sin and provide the opportunity for salvation.

During the Good Friday **liturgy**, four main things happen:

- the **passion** of Jesus is read in full, often with the congregation enacting the part of the crowd
- crucifixes are venerated by the congregation
- the priest preaches a sermon about the meaning of salvation
- Holy Communion is distributed from the tabernacle (a container for the bread and wine) – it will have been consecrated the night before at the Holy Thursday service.

The Easter vigil

Late on the evening of Holy Saturday, a very long service begins, often outside the church beside a bonfire. Fire represents a naturally occurring event but is also a powerful source of light. Catholics believe that Jesus' death and resurrection brought light into the world. A large **Paschal** candle is lit from the fire and is always re-lit for Mass and for baptisms. The congregation then light their candles from the Paschal candle or from each other to symbolise Christ's light passing through the Church. It represents Jesus as the light of the world. During the Easter vigil other symbolic actions occur:

- readings from the Old Testament are repeated to record the prophecies of Jesus' saving work
- prayers are said for the salvation of all the people in the world
- the waters of baptism are blessed
- new converts are admitted to the Church.

All these acts can take place at other times of the year, but they have a special meaning at Easter.

Devout Catholics will attend all three ceremonies that comprise the Easter Triduum. They may also attend the 'Stations of the Cross' in the morning or evening of Good Friday (see Topic 4.2).

REMEMBER THIS

'Venerate' means worship. It can take many forms, but on Good Friday veneration takes the form of members of the congregation kissing the feet of a statue of Jesus on a crucifix.

The Paschal candle is lit at mass on Holy Saturday.

AO2 skills ACTIVITIES

Assess why Easter is considered the most important Christian festival. With your work partner write a script with one of you defending Christmas and the other Easter. Role-play it to other members of the class.

Festivals 2: Christmas and Advent

The next two pages will help you to:

- understand why Christmas is a special time for Catholics
- explain the beliefs that support the festival of Christmas
- explain that Advent is also an important part of Christmas
- make a statement with evidence outlining your views on Christmas.

Advent

Four Sundays before **Christmas**, in every Catholic parish, a candle on an **Advent** wreath will be lit to mark the countdown to Christmas. In order to mark off the days, children may open the doors on an Advent calendar.

Advent calendars are used to count down the days to Christmas.

AO1 skills ACTIVITIES

Create a mind map of one major Christian festival. Remember to include its origins, Bible passages, customs and beliefs. Illustrate your page with appropriate signs and symbols.

MUST THINK ABOUT!

Catholics, along with all other Christians, believe that Jesus was God. This is a miracle. It is hard to imagine the creator of the Universe as a tiny baby, in the arms of its mother. Perhaps this is what Catholics find so inspiring – Jesus, God and man, lying in a manger.

AO1 skills ACTIVITIES

In 1647 celebrating Christmas in England was banned (see page 37). What benefits might there be if this law was brought back today? Share your ideas with your work partner.

Advent has a two-fold purpose: it reminds people of the wait for Christ's birth or **incarnation**, and when God took human form and lived in the world. This is an event worthy of celebration and so it is not surprising that big parties are planned. Families join up at Christmas because it is seen as a time for being together with loved ones. One model for this was the Holy Family of Nazareth: Mary, Joseph and Jesus.

From 'Once in Royal David's City'

He came down to earth from heaven,
who is God and Lord of all,
and his shelter was a stable,
and his cradle was a stall;
with the poor and meek and lowly,
lived on earth, our Saviour holy.
Mrs Alexander (1818–1895)

Christmas

Some Christians will go to **Mass** at midnight on Christmas Eve. This has a very special atmosphere. Others may choose to go at dawn and recreate the actions of the shepherds, who were guarding their sheep in the hills, but who were encouraged to go and find a saviour by a whole host of angels.

On Christmas Day, Catholics are expected to go to Mass, where the readings will be from the stories of Jesus' birth (the Infancy Narratives).

Some churches will have a family Mass, during which the children are encouraged to give away a toy that they no longer need so that it can be given to a less fortunate family. Some will visit the needy, housebound or lonely to ensure that everyone can enjoy the benefits of such a great day.

The crib

It is very common for Catholic churches to provide a crib scene which can become the focus for worship as people are invited to reflect on the poverty into which Jesus was born. In the crib there are usually statues of Mary, Joseph and the baby Jesus. The figure of Jesus is usually added during Midnight Mass to symbolise the arrival of Jesus in the middle of the night. Statues of an ox and ass may also be found there, as these animals are said to have witnessed his birth.

AO2 skills ACTIVITIES

Consider the idea that Christmas is for children and Easter is for adults. If this were really the case what difference would it make? Explore the ways in which Easter could be made more accessible for children.

AO2 skills ACTIVITIES

Imagine you work for a publicity agency. The local Catholic church approaches your company to create either a leaflet or a PowerPoint presentation to highlight the benefits of celebrating events in the life of Jesus together. With your work partner draw up a set of arguments which should be included.

Special days: saints' days and Sunday

The next two pages will help you to:

- describe why Sunday is a special day for Catholics
- explain the importance of saints' days for Catholics.

Papier-mâché figures made for the Día de los Muertos – Day of the Dead – celebrations in Los Angeles, California. The Day of the Dead takes place from 31 October until 2 November.

Why Sunday?

Catholics share Sunday as their day of rest with most of the rest of Christianity. This is to remind them of their core belief that Jesus rose from the dead on 'the first day of the week'. Jews start the week at sunset on Saturday so for the apostles, the first day of the week was Sunday.

One Christian denomination celebrates the **Sabbath** by having their day of rest on Saturday. These people are Seventh Day Adventists.

AO1 skills ACTIVITIES

Explain what you understand by the phrase 'Communion of Saints' (refer back to Topic 1.9). Saints do not necessarily have to have been perfect – they just need to have been people who tried to live Christ-like lives. Whose names would be on a list of your favourite top ten saints? Give reasons for three of your choices.

Keeping Sunday special

Every Catholic is expected to attend **Mass** on Sunday. In the past it was seen as a sin to miss Mass. Today, some Catholics wish to emphasise the reasons for keeping Sunday special, and for them, Sunday is a time for:

- an inspiring and uplifting celebration of the Eucharist, and for personal prayer
- being with the family – many use the time to visit relatives or friends
- recreation (literally recreating yourself).

Saints' days

Throughout the Church's calendar a number of days are set aside to celebrate the lives of the holy women and men of the Church. Those whose lives do not have particular relevance to the local community are brought to mind on All Saints' Day (1 November). Everyone else who was a Christian in their lifetime is remembered on All Souls' Day (2 November).

Well-known saints

Some of the saints' days that have become part of British culture are:

- St Swithun's Day (15 July) – a day used to forecast the weather
- St Stephen's Day (26 December) – now more commonly known as Boxing Day and often a day for visiting family
- St Valentine's Day (14 February) – a day to celebrate romance.

Patron saints

A patron saint is a saint who is considered to have a special relationship with a particular group or church and who can intercede or plead on their behalf. The idea of a patron saint is not unique to Catholicism. In families, schools or churches where there is a patron saint, there will often be a shrine to that person, including a statue or image. On the 'patronal' feast this may be decorated with flowers, and a prayer service may be held at the shrine. It is common for people to make a special effort to go to Mass on the feast day.

If the saint is known for something particular, this is usually commemorated on their feast day. For example, on St Blaise's Day (3 February), there is a ceremony called 'the blessing of the throats' that recalls the miracle he performed when a child got a fishbone stuck in his throat.

There may be a school in your town that is named after a saint. Catholic schools which are named after a saint may well have a special patronal feast on which this person is remembered.

MUST THINK ABOUT!

Sabbath practice is inherited from the Jewish origins of Christianity. The Hebrew word is *Shabbat* and means 'day of rest'. It occurs on Saturday as this is the seventh day of the week and was the day on which God rested after creating the Universe (see Genesis 1). Orthodox Jews will make sure they live no more than a 'Sabbath's walk' from the synagogue so that they only have to make a short journey to worship and can spend the rest of the time in prayer or sharing family life.

AO2 skills ACTIVITIES

Recent laws have made Sunday similar to other days. What do you think are the effects of these changes on the practice of faith? Write, in about 500 words, what Sunday should be like in order for young Catholics to feel supported in their faith.

AO2 skills ACTIVITIES

If God needed someone to reveal an important message for the salvation of his people today, do you think he would choose a young person, a celebrity or a religious leader? Prepare a one-minute speech to be read out to the rest of the class giving reasons for your choice.

Topic 2.5

Pilgrimages

The next two pages will help you to:

- describe what happens on a Catholic pilgrimage
- explain why Catholics undertake pilgrimages
- outline your own thoughts about the value of participating in pilgrimage.

The history of pilgrimages

As contestants leave the *X Factor* or other reality television shows, they remark frequently that they have 'been on a journey'. This is a well-known human phenomenon. The Exodus story in the Bible is the story of the journey of the whole Jewish people. Every Muslim is expected to visit Makkah once during their lifetime to make the Hajj. Consider the collection of stories written by Geoffrey Chaucer towards the end of the Middle Ages known as the *Canterbury Tales*. Each of the tales related to a fictional pilgrim on their way to the shrine of St Thomas à Becket in Canterbury (see Topics 2.8 and 3.10).

People make journeys or **pilgrimages** such as these for non-religious reasons too. For example, there are many people from all over the world who will make a journey to Liverpool to see the places that are associated with the Beatles or to see Anfield, the home of Liverpool Football Club.

AO1 skills **ACTIVITIES**

The Catholic Church refers to itself as 'a pilgrim church' and often refers to life as a journey. Describe how and explain why the Church uses these particular words.

The Grotto shrine of Our Lady of Lourdes.

Jesus' own journey

A careful reading of the gospels suggests that Jesus made his own journey through Galilee, then across the Jordan valley and out of Israel, then back into Israel and down into Jerusalem. During this time Jesus spent some days alone praying in the wilderness, and eventually made his way to the Temple in Jerusalem.

Mark 11:15–18

So they reached Jerusalem and he went into the Temple and began driving out the men selling and buying there; he upset the tables of the money changers and the seats of the dove sellers. Nor would he allow anyone to carry anything through the Temple. And he taught them and said, 'Does not scripture say: My house will be called a house of prayer for all peoples? But you have turned it into a bandits' den.' This came to the ears of the chief priests and the scribes, and they tried to find some way of doing away with him; they were afraid of him because the people were carried away by his teaching.

In Matthew's account of Jesus' birth there is also the story of Mary and Joseph taking him into Egypt to escape the persecution of King Herod (See Matthew 2).

Catholics and pilgrimages

Making a pilgrimage is not compulsory for Catholics, but there are many who undertake them voluntarily. Like Jesus, many make the journey to Jerusalem. Here they can see the places associated with Jesus' story. Pilgrimages to the Holy Land are organised by parishes, dioceses or private individuals. In addition, many Catholics like to make a pilgrimage to Rome to experience the magnificence of the Vatican or to spend some time retracing the steps of the apostles, most notably Peter.

Indulgences gained by pilgrimage

In 2008, Pope Benedict XVI granted a modern indulgence for pilgrims visiting Lourdes. (An indulgence is a lessening of the time spent in Purgatory and is granted by the Pope.) This was to mark the 150th anniversary of St Bernadette's visions of Mary, the Immaculate Conception. Each person was to visit each of the important sites in the town, praying the rosary and joining in with religious activities. This was just like the medieval pilgrims in Chaucer's tales, trying to store up future blessings.

AO2 skills ACTIVITIES

'Spending time and money going on a pilgrimage is a selfish thing to do.' Write a conversation between two people, one who supports this view and one who disagrees.

FOR INTEREST

Medieval pilgrims used to roam across Europe visiting sites associated with miracles or important people. One of those places is Santiago di Compostela in northern Spain. To get there from Rome meant crossing the Alps and Pyrenees. Lourdes was an important staging post on this journey long before Bernadette's vision made it globally significant for Catholics.

AO2 skills ACTIVITIES

Catholics believe that visiting holy places can help heal, if not cure, those with sickness and disease. Create a leaflet to promote a visit to a place of pilgrimage. It needs to include details of the origin of the place, a description of what is on offer and evidence based on real-life accounts of people who have returned home feeling better in some way.

Places to do with Jesus

The next two pages will help you to:

- identify some of the places associated with the accounts of Jesus' life
- explain what happened at each of these sites of pilgrimage
- evaluate pilgrimage as a way of understanding the life and times of Jesus.

Bethlehem

Made famous by the **Christmas** story, the town of Bethlehem is known to many people. At the time of Jesus, it was known as the town of David, since it was the ancestral home of the most famous of all the Kings of Israel. Its relevance to the story of Jesus is that it locates him in the royal line as far back as Jesse, David's father. Did this make Jesus the 'King of the Jews'? There is no record that this is how Jesus saw himself, nor of Jesus' actual place of birth. Even the details vary between the gospels.

In the 2nd century CE Justin Martyr wrote that Jesus was born in a 'cave close to the village'. This cave is where the Church of the Nativity now stands.

Luke 2:4–5

So Joseph set out from the town of Nazareth in Galilee for Judaea, to David's town called Bethlehem, since he was of David's house and line, in order to be registered together with Mary, his betrothed, who was with child.

AO1 skills ACTIVITIES

Make a list of all the places of pilgrimage that are associated with Jesus and describe one in detail. Prepare a short talk on your chosen place, giving reasons why your class should consider visiting it.

Nazareth

To get to Bethlehem Joseph would have had to take Mary nearly the whole length of Israel from his home in Nazareth. This would have been an epic journey in its time on foot. Joseph seems to have undertaken this for two reasons:

- to fulfil the Jewish prophecies that the Messiah or saviour would be born in Bethlehem
- the Romans commanded all their citizens to go back to their family's home town in order to be registered.

Important sites in Nazareth are:

- the Synagogue Church in Nazareth, which is built on the traditional site of the synagogue where Jesus preached (see Luke 4:16)
- the Church of Joseph, which stands on the traditional site of Joseph's carpentry shop
- the Mensa Christi ('Table of Christ') Church, which stands where tradition says that Jesus ate with the apostles after the resurrection
- the Basilica of Jesus the Adolescent on a hill above the city.

A modern map of the State of Israel.

Galilee

The Sea of Galilee (sometimes referred to by its Roman name Lake Tiberias) is mentioned frequently in the early part of each of the gospels. There are some towns mentioned that are close by, such as Capernaum, which may have been the home of the apostles Peter, Andrew, James and John, who were fishermen.

Catholic pilgrims achieve a real sense of the closeness of Jesus when they visit these places because the stories are so familiar. Imagine walking alongside the water on which Jesus himself miraculously walked or where he calmed the storm. Imagine sailing across the water in a boat not dissimilar to that from which he famously preached because there were too many people thronging the shore. Imagine fishing the same waters that he used as a metaphor to explain to the apostles that their task in the Church would be to catch new souls.

Jerusalem

Jerusalem today is very different from the time of Jesus. The Romans destroyed Herod's Temple in 70 CE. All that remains is the Western Wall, known as the Wailing Wall, which has become a special place of **pilgrimage** for Jews. The influence of Islam is very strong, as Jerusalem is also a place of pilgrimage for Muslims reliving the life and times of the prophet Muhammad ﷺ.

Catholic pilgrims will make a special 'way of the cross' along the Via Dolorosa which means 'the way of sadness'. This marks the route that Jesus may have taken from Pilate's Palace to Calvary, the place of execution. On each sacred site the Church has built a lasting shrine or monument, usually enclosed in a church building. Here the edges between history, archaeology and religion become blurred.

There are many other places of pilgrimage in Jerusalem, such as the Garden of Gethsemane and the Church of the Holy Sepulchure, which is said to be built over the cave where Jesus' body was placed after his death. Other Christians believe he was buried in the Garden Tomb on the Mount of Olives.

There are also the Church of St Anne (Mary's mother), the Cathedral of St James, the Tomb of the Virgin, the Church of St Stephen and the Church of St Mary on the Temple hill, as well as the Upper Room.

RESEARCH NOTE

Write an account of what happened to Jesus when he made a pilgrimage at the age of 12 to Jerusalem (Luke 2:41–50). What evidence is there in the story to show that this event was a turning point in his life? Give reasons why going on a pilgrimage today might change someone's life.

FOR DEBATE

Pilgrimages are not a compulsory part of Christianity, but many Catholics believe that they strengthen their faith and deepen their understanding. Explore the reasons why some believers think this and discuss other religious practices which might be more helpful.

AO2 skills ACTIVITIES

The Emmaus story (Luke 24:13ff) suggests that Jesus met people in their everyday lives. Assess the reasons why some Catholics feel it is necessary to go to places Jesus once visited to feel closer to him. Compare answers with your work partner, and then write a paragraph including the strongest reasons.

Places of pilgrimage associated with Mary

The next two pages will help you to:

- identify some of the places of pilgrimage connected with Mary
- explain why these places are significant for Catholics
- make an informed judgement on the value of pilgrimage for Catholics.

Our Lady of Lourdes

In south-western France there is a shrine called Our Lady of Lourdes. It is believed that Mary, in the form of the Immaculate Conception, appeared to a young woman, Bernadette Soubirous, at Lourdes in 1858. Every year thousands of Catholics, and other interested people, visit Lourdes for a spiritual experience which includes visits to the Grotto where a spring was discovered by Bernadette, Stations of the Cross, meditations on the rosary, bathing in the healing waters of the spring, candle-lit processions, and as many **Masses** as a person wishes to hear. Pilgrims can also visit important sites relating to the life of Bernadette.

Guadalupe

Mary is also said to have appeared to another young person, Juan Diego, a Mexican of humble origins, on a hill called Tepeyac near Mexico City in 1531. St Juan Diego reported his vision as Our Lady of Guadalupe and this seems to have inspired the Catholic faith of the people of Mexico. The Basilica of Guadalupe, built to commemorate these events, is one of the world's most visited shrines. It houses an ancient relic supposed to have been the apron worn by Juan Diego on which appeared an image of Our Lady of Guadalupe. This relic is still intact today.

Catholics visiting Guadalupe pray the rosary, hear Mass, light candles and kneel in prayer at the shrine.

Fátima

Mary also appeared several times to three young peasant children at Fátima in Portugal in 1917. Luciá dos Santos, the main visionary, died in 2005, but was kept hidden from the world because of the predictions that she is said to have received from Mary about what would happen in the future. Fátima is a special place for pilgrims because Mary appeared repeatedly – a breakthrough from the spiritual world.

AO1 skills ACTIVITIES

Many Catholic mothers have a great devotion to Mary. Describe how this devotion can be seen in practice and explain why many Catholics choose to visit a Marian shrine.

MUST THINK ABOUT!

The technical word for an appearance from the spirit world is 'apparition'. In most cases, the apparition is only seen by the recipient (the person experiencing the vision). Those who receive these apparitions report the contents to those who will listen and usually they pass them on to a local priest. The priest will notify the authorities so that the authenticity of the event can be investigated.

AO1 skills ACTIVITIES

Make an ideas map of the places of pilgrimage associated with Mary. Choose one Marian site, describe its origins and explain what happens there nowadays. Give reasons why you might or might not visit the place yourself.

Knock

On the 21 August 1879 it is said that an apparition occurred on the south gable of the parish church of Knock in the west of Ireland. On this occasion, Mary is said to have appeared with St Joseph and St John the Evangelist. Knock is now the most important shrine in Ireland, and thousands of people make **pilgrimages** there every year. A popular pilgrimage time is from 15 August (the Feast of the Assumption) to 21 August, the anniversary of the apparitions.

REMEMBER THIS

The immaculate conception is the Roman Catholic teaching that the Virgin Mary was conceived by her mother, St Anne, without any stain of original sin (see p. 5).
She was filled with the grace of God and lived her life without any sin.

Marian shrines in England

A shrine dedicated to Mary, Our Lady, the Immaculate Conception or the Mother of God is called a Marian shrine. There are two in England – Walsingham in Norfolk and Aylesford Priory in Kent.

Walsingham is often referred to as 'England's Nazareth'. In 1061 CE, the Lady Richeldis, whose husband owned the manor, had a vision of the Virgin Mary in which she was told to rebuild Mary's house in Nazareth at Walsingham. She did this and it has been a centre of pilgrimage since that time.

The priory of Walsingham was destroyed in 1538 when Henry VIII ordered the dissolution of the monasteries. In 1897 Catholic pilgrimage to Walsingham was resumed to a building outside the village known as the Slipper Chapel (the Chapel of St Catherine of Alexandria). The building contains a statue of Our Lady of Walsingham that is based on the image on the Priory seal.

Aylesford Priory, Kent.

Luke 2:16–19

So they hurried away and found Mary and Joseph, and the baby lying in the manger. When they saw the child they repeated what they had been told about him, and everyone who heard it was astonished at what the shepherds said to them. As for Mary, she treasured all these things and pondered them in her heart.

AO2 skills ACTIVITIES

Since the early years of the Church, Mary has been known by many titles, one of them being 'Mother of God'. What arguments would you put forward to someone who said that Catholics worshipped Mary as though she were more important than Jesus?

Places of pilgrimage associated with saints

The next two pages will help you to:

- identify some of the places of pilgrimage connected with saints
- explain why these places are significant for Catholics
- develop an informed view on the value of pilgrimage for Catholics.

Basilica of St Francis in Assisi.

Canterbury

St Thomas à Becket was Archbishop of Canterbury in 12th-century England. He opposed King Henry II's interference in the running of the Church and was murdered by assassins in Canterbury Cathedral. Although Canterbury is now an Anglican Cathedral, at the time of Thomas it was part of the Catholic Church and was possibly the most important building in England. After Thomas's martyrdom many people made the **pilgrimage** to Canterbury, many of them hoping to receive cures by simply touching his tomb.

AO1 skills ACTIVITIES

Consider what makes a person a saint. Using ten cards write the name of a different saint on one side and clues to their identity on the back. In turn you and your work partner should question each other to see how many saints you can identify from your clues. Explain why some were easier and others harder to work out.

Assisi

One of the best-known and favourite saints of the Catholic Church is St Francis of Assisi. He is famed for:

- founding the Franciscan religious order
- instituting the practice of having a crib depict the nativity scene at **Christmas** time
- his love and care for animals.

Francis is remembered in his home town of Assisi in Italy, which is visited by many pilgrims.

Extract from the Prayer of St Francis

Make me a channel of your peace,
Where there is hatred let me bring your love;
Where there is injury your pardon, Lord;
And where there's doubt, true faith in you.

Santiago di Compostela

Santiago di Compostela is an important shrine sited in Galicia in north-west Spain. Santiago gets its name from St James, one of the apostles, whose tomb was discovered in the 9th century in this place, a long way from Jerusalem. Pilgrims have visited this site ever since, making the journey to get close to one of Jesus' closest companions.

The location of James's tomb is now the site of a magnificent cathedral that took over 50 years to build.

MUST THINK ABOUT!

Consider for a moment the impact of having an insight from God about how the world is to be. Imagine telling all your friends about it. How do you think they would react? Would they accept that what you were telling was the truth or would they take a different view? How would you convince them that you were not making it up?

Ávila and Lisieux

Other European Catholic centres of pilgrimage can be found at Ávila in Spain and Lisieux in France, which were home to St Theresa (Ávila) and St Thérèse (Lisieux). These two women are regarded by the Church as having great spiritual insight.

St Theresa of Ávila formed some very important ideas that are used by Catholics today in their spiritual development. She also founded a religious order known as the Discalced Carmelites. The Carmelites are a contemplative order, who pray for the conversion of the world and attempt to develop spiritual enlightenment.

St Thérèse of Lisieux was known for more simple approaches to faith, including her idea that Catholics should celebrate the power of God in the most humble of pastimes, such as doing the washing-up. She believed that it should all be dedicated to the Lord.

Catholic pilgrims to these sites seek inspiration and offer their own devotions to these women who left their mark on the history of Christianity. The Basilica at Lisieux contains the 'elbow' of Thérèse as a permanent relic to her time in this town. Like the tomb of St Thomas à Becket at Canterbury, some pilgrims seek healing from their proximity to it. Many will sit in quiet prayer contemplating the stories of these people.

AO2 skills ACTIVITIES

Organise a balloon debate with four of the most popular and well-known saints in the basket of a hot-air balloon. Contribute reasons to ensure the saint you think is the most worthy will not be thrown out of the sinking balloon.

Devotion to the saints suggests an understanding of and a belief in the afterlife. Examine whether or not there is any value in making a pilgrimage if you do not believe in life after death.

Rome

One of the most popular places of Catholic pilgrimage is the Vatican City in Rome. According to tradition, the altar of the Basilica of St Peter stands over the grave of the crucified St Peter. Of course, Rome is also of great importance because it is the home of the Pope.

Places of prayer for Catholics

The next two pages will help you to:

- identify some of the places of pilgrimage connected with prayer in the Catholic tradition
- explain why these places are significant for Catholics
- develop an informed view on the value of pilgrimage, retreat and spiritual development for Catholics.

The Abbey Church of St Mary, Iona.

Iona

Like Jesus, some of the great founding fathers of Christianity went to very remote places to find the space and peace to pray and get close to God. One such place is Iona in Western Scotland, just off the island of Mull. This is one of the oldest surviving sites of British Christianity. Pilgrims make their journey to Iona to share in the prayerful traditions of one of the most ancient monastic communities. The Iona community supports the pilgrims by feeding them and providing shelter. Today this ecumenical community (a place where members of different Christian denominations come together) has a commitment to justice and working for the environment.

You can read about the Iona community online.

AO1 skills ACTIVITIES

Choose one place of pilgrimage dedicated to prayer and worship. Describe how and explain why it is different from other places of pilgrimage.

Kintbury

A more recent (1975) Catholic community set up to provide **pilgrimage** space for prayer and reflection is the De La Salle community of St Cassian's at Kintbury in Berkshire. The De La Salle religious order was founded by St John the Baptist de la Salle, with a commitment to education. St Cassian's mainly focuses on young people but also caters for families wishing to make a retreat together. There are also retreats aimed at adults wishing to get some time away from their busy working lives.

Taizé

During the Second World War a young man called Roger established a community at a place called Taizé in south-east France to house refugees, particularly Jews. After the war, as a gesture of reconciliation and forgiveness, it became an ecumenical centre, which welcomes pilgrims from all over the world and from any denomination. Some people choose to stay on and join the community. Others visit only for a short time for spiritual uplifting and refreshment. Some call this a retreat as they 'retreat' from the world to spend some time in reflection.

Catholics make up a proportion of the people who visit Taizé each year, often returning because of their enjoyment of the particular form of meditative worship that characterises the place. Repetitive chants are sung, which allow pilgrims to focus on a simple idea and to try to make sense of it in their own lives. Many of these are sung in Latin, the universal language of Christianity.

Croagh Patrick

One of the most powerful Catholic religious devotions is the pilgrimage to Croagh Patrick in County Mayo in Ireland. Croagh Patrick is a mountain that rises out of the countryside and dominates the skyline for miles around. It is named after St Patrick who is reputed to have taken Christianity to Ireland and converted the Celtic people from paganism. There is a small chapel at the top of the mountain, which is used for **Mass** by the thousands of pilgrims who make the climb on the last Sunday in July. Many of them climb the rugged mountain on their knees as a sign of their humility.

Prayer on Croagh Patrick may be aided by religious objects like rosaries and crucifixes, but it is the physical work of climbing that says the most about a person's faith.

MUST THINK ABOUT!

A pilgrimage is a special time of personal prayer and reflection. Each pilgrim uses the time to renew their relationship with God. They may gain other benefits from making the journey, but the main reason is their spiritual improvement.

AO1 skills ACTIVITIES

Decorate a page in your book with all the Christian places associated with prayer where pilgrims may visit. Next to the name, label or draw signs and symbols which best describe and explain its history and present-day customs.

FOR DEBATE

Residential retreats in school time to religious communities such as the De La Salle Brothers at Kintbury have grown in popularity. What arguments would you put forward to your headteacher to show that the benefits to the individuals and to the school community outweigh the time lost in the classroom?

AO2 skills ACTIVITIES

Communities of prayer, for instance Taizé, advise pilgrims to stay for at least a week in order to experience fully what is on offer. Examine the strengths and weaknesses of having to commit this amount of time.

Effects and benefits of pilgrimages

The next two pages will help you to:

- identify the benefits of making a pilgrimage
- explain why pilgrimage remains a popular way of celebrating Catholic life
- make a balanced presentation of your own views on pilgrimage.

Pilgrims at Croagh Patrick.

Short-term benefits

A group returning home from a **pilgrimage** will tell of the good times they have had. They will report the spiritual uplift they have received and they may also report the difficulties they faced. Initially they will have experienced a sense of euphoria (great happiness or well-being), which often comes from spending time with a group of like-minded people. In addition to this they may feel:

- inspired to renew their commitment to the Church and to the practice of their faith
- motivated to become more involved in good works
- challenged to keep up their new religious commitment
- frustrated by the apathy or lack of energy they experience away from the pilgrimage.

AO1 skills ACTIVITIES

With your work partner create a pilgrimage board game similar to Snakes and Ladders. What difficulties or challenges would have to happen to take you back to the starting point, or, alternatively, lead you to feeling closer to God after you had completed your pilgrimage?

FOR DEBATE

'The money could have been better spent providing hot food for the old people of the parish.' In groups, develop a five minute presentation for the rest of the class making a response to this statement that was once made about a parish pilgrimage.

Maintaining the prayerful life may be the hardest part of all. This is because it is easy to find time to pray when every other aspect of life is catered for. When the everyday struggles of life get in the way it is hard to find the time to sit still and pray.

The emotional response to a pilgrimage can be very powerful. A pilgrimage can be a roller-coaster experience, with sensational highs and very deep lows. For this reason pilgrims may return home more tired than when they went away. A parish pilgrimage can be the catalyst for a period of renewal in the Church as enthusiasm sweeps through the community. If this is harnessed it can be a positive force for the development of all members. A diocesan pilgrimage can also be a positive opportunity to build links across a region and with different groups within it.

Long-term benefits

For Christians, the renewal of a person's faith can be helpful at any stage or time of life. If this is triggered by a visit to somewhere like the Holy Land or Rome, then the effort can be seen to have been worth it. Every experience is a learning experience so a pilgrimage is bound to create new knowledge, skills or understanding for the pilgrim, which they might not recognise immediately. In years to come, pilgrims may also realise the benefits of the experience in an unexpected way.

The work of an organisation like HCPT (The Pilgrimage Trust), a Catholic group set up to provide opportunities for sick or disabled children to go on pilgrimage, can have many lasting benefits for both the pilgrims and their carers. One of the most positive outcomes might be the development of lasting friendships between them. In addition, a form of healing may take place which, although not a direct cure, might bring peace of mind to the pilgrim as they come to terms with their condition. Recognising that others suffer can be the beginning of someone accepting pain in their own life.

AO1 skills ACTIVITIES

Describe and explain the possible short- and long-term benefits of making a pilgrimage. Pool your ideas with your work partner and share your views with the class.

AO2 skills ACTIVITIES

Taizé offers its retreatants the opportunity to spend the week apart, in separate quarters and in silence, with like-minded young people. A minority of visitors take up this offer; the rest prefer to study and learn together in groups. Account for why some value the silence, whereas the majority do not.

MUST THINK ABOUT!

There are many travel companies that specialise in enabling pilgrims to complete their journey successfully. For them this is a commercial venture. What do you think Jesus would have said about this? Would he have approved? How could it be organised on a different basis? Talk this through with teachers or other students working on Business and Enterprise initiatives in your school.

AO2 skills ACTIVITIES

Making a pilgrimage is not a compulsory part of Christianity, but many Catholics believe it strengthens their faith. Examine whether or not a really good holiday would have the same beneficial effects.

GradeStudio

Welcome to the Grade Studio

GCSE is about what you can do, not what you can't do. You need to know what examiners want in your answers so that you can get the best possible marks. In GCSE Religious Studies there are two things that examiners are looking for. These are called assessment objectives (AO). Questions are designed to help examiners find out how well you do in each assessment objective.

Graded examples for this topic

AO1

AO1 questions test what you know and how well you can explain and analyse things. Let's look at some AO1 questions to see what examiners are expecting you to do.

Question

Why is Sunday special for Christians? **[6 marks]**

Although the word 'explain' is not in the question that is what you are being asked to do. To achieve the highest level, you should try to give three good reasons for Sunday being special for Christians.

Student's answer	Examiner's comment
Jesus rose from the dead on Sunday so Christians believe it is special. Catholics go to Mass on this day and many Christians gather together as a family.	The candidate has given an accurate answer but it lacks the necessary detail and explanation to achieve beyond Level 1.

Student's answer	Examiner's comment
Christians believe that Jesus rising from the dead is the most important part of their faith. Many Christians avoid shopping on this day, although the shops are now open. There is a long tradition of resting from work because in the book of Genesis God rested on the Sabbath. For Jews the Sabbath is celebrated on Saturday but for Christians the Sabbath is celebrated on Sunday as Jesus rose on this day.	The candidate has written a satisfactory answer because they have made a link between the Jewish and Christian traditions, both of whom use the Old Testament as a source of authority. The candidate now needs to draw out the reasons (Level 2).

Student's improved answer	Examiner's comment
Sundays are special for Christians because Jesus rose from the dead on Easter Sunday, which proved that he was the Son of God and that there is an afterlife. For Catholics every Sunday should be a celebration like a mini Easter day and should be spent differently from any other day of the week because in the Bible (Genesis) God rested on the Sabbath. Catholics attend Mass on a Sunday, and other Christians spend time in church and at home reading the Bible and resting from work. This pattern is repeated in many other religions, such as Judaism. Christians believe spending Sunday like this helps them in many ways. It helps them focus on what really matters in their lives, and gives them time to go to church to worship God and time to be with their families. Often they will share Sunday lunch together.	The candidate has written a good answer because they have included and developed the Christian beliefs about Sunday and linked it with other religions, customs and practices (Level 3).

AO2

Question

Christmas is more important to Catholics than Easter. **[12 marks]**

AO2 questions are worth 50 per cent of the marks for each question, so you must practise expressing other people's views and develop you own view and support it with evidence.

You also need to practise holding back from expressing your own view until you have explained and made a comments about the views of others.

Often candidates lose marks because they focus too much on their own view, forgetting to express other views. This limits what might otherwise be a good response to Level 1 or Level 2.

Student's answer

Easter is more important because it celebrates the event of the resurrection of Jesus, which is the key belief of Christians.

Examiner's comment

The candidate has given a reasonable answer but only gives one point of view (Level 1).

Student's answer

Easter is more important because it celebrates the event of the resurrection of Jesus, which is the key belief of Christians. However, some people might think that Christmas is the more important festival because it is more popular and because it celebrates the birth of Jesus the saviour.

Examiner's comment

The candidate has written a reasonable answer giving two points of view. They now need to give a personal view and support it (Level 2).

Student's improved answer

Easter is more important because it celebrates the event of the resurrection of Jesus, which is the key belief of Christians. However, some people might think that Christmas is the more important festival because it is more popular and because it celebrates the birth of Jesus the saviour. I think that they are equally important, but are celebrated differently. Although Christmas is more popular and celebrated more by the public, this does not make it more important to Christians. They are equally significant and the faith could not exist without either event.

Examiner's comment

This is now a good answer to the question with two supported viewpoints and a personal view which is also supported (Level 4).

These specimen answers provide an outline of how you could construct your response. Space does not allow us to give a full response. The examiner will be looking for more detail in your actual exam responses.

Remember and Reflect

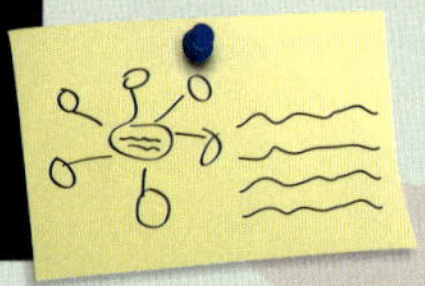

AO1 Describe, explain and analyse, using knowledge and understanding

	Find the answer on:
1 Explain in simple terms what is meant by the liturgical calendar.	PAGE 38
2 Other than Christmas and Easter, name four important Catholic festivals.	PAGE 38
3 For each of the four festivals named in question 2 explain their significance for Catholics and the events that they celebrate.	PAGE 38–39
4 List the six other holy days of celebration for Catholic Christians living in England.	PAGE 39
5 Describe in detail the three parts of the Catholic Triduum.	PAGE 40–41
6 In which Jewish festival does Easter have its origins?	PAGE 38
7 What does the Paschal candle used at the Holy Saturday liturgy represent?	PAGE 41
8 Give other examples of when light or fire is used in Catholic worship.	PAGE49
9 Explain why turkeys, Christmas trees and tinsel have become accepted parts of Catholic worship, even though they are not mentioned in the New Testament.	PAGE 42–43
10 For what reason is Sunday a special day for Catholics?	PAGE 44–45
11 What is a patronal feast day?	PAGE 45
12 What is a pilgrimage?	PAGE 37
13 Make a list of five important places of pilgrimage for Catholics.	PAGE 48–53
14 Which global place of pilgrimage is shared by Catholics, other Christians, Jews and Muslims?	PAGE 49
15 Explain the significance of Galilee for Catholics.	PAGE 49
16 Retell the story of Juan Diego of Mexico.	PAGE 50
17 Explain what happens at Kintbury.	PAGE 55
18 How would Catholics in the Middle Ages travel to places like Santiago di Compostela in northern Spain?	PAGE 47
19 What effect is pilgrimage believed to have on a Catholic's life?	PAGE 47

AO2 Use evidence and reasoned argument to express and evaluate personal responses, informed insights, and differing viewpoints

1. For hundreds of years pilgrims have made the climb to the top of the holy mountain, Croagh Patrick, many of them on their knees. Do you have the kind of faith that would inspire you to make such a journey? Is there anything for which you would be prepared to make such a commitment? Support your answer with reasons.
2. Catholics are expected to go to Mass every Sunday. Do you think this realistic, reasonable or responsible in the 21st century? Explain the thinking behind your answers.
3. Consider the following statement from an anonymous policeman: 'Christmas is the most miserable time of the year: we get called to more domestics than at any other time of the year; many people get so drunk their kids are neglected; there is a higher than normal rate of prank calls to 999 and for some children the whole thing is made worse because they have to spend it with relatives they don't even like. I'm not sure this is what Jesus would have wanted.' How do you react to this statement? Write a detailed analysis of the quote from your own point of view.
4. Do you agree that 'Good Friday' was given the right name? Give reasons for your answer.
5. Write a letter to your local Catholic Church explaining why you think it is important that they hold a birthday party on Pentecost. Use evidence from the Acts of the Apostles to support your argument.
6. Palestine? Israel? Holy Land? Which name best describes for you the territory that was Jesus' homeland? Explain the reasons for your answer by drawing on historical sources.
7. Name a place that is special to you. Write about why it is special or significant in your life. Give at least three reasons. If you can, recall significant events that occurred there and explain why these have become important for you.
8. Thousands of Catholics flock to Lourdes in France every year. Explain why they do this. Do you think they are wasting their time? Set out your argument, with reasons.

Topic 3: Major divisions and interpretations

The Big Picture

In this Topic you will be examining:

- a short history of Christianity
- the major divisions between Catholicism and other Christian traditions
- some of the different expressions of Catholicism around the world
- those things that are shared by all Christians across the world.

What?

You will:

- study some important moments in the history of Christianity
- look at the lives and works of some important characters in that history
- explore the differences between Catholicism and some of the other traditions within Christianity
- explore the diversity of cultural expressions of Catholicism.

Why?

Because:

- knowing about the history of Christianity helps to give context to the present-day situation
- the stories of important people within the history of Catholicism help us to understand the issues they faced
- knowing and understanding the differences between Catholics and other Christians helps to explain why customs, traditions and practices can vary
- knowing about diverse Catholic cultures from around the world helps to explain the global nature of Catholicism.

How?

By:

- an investigative approach to the history of Christianity
- examining sources and commentaries on historical events
- studying the words and writings of different Christian groups
- exploring the cultural context of different expressions of Catholicism.

The Most Reverend Dr Rowan Williams, Archbishop of Canterbury (left) meets His Holiness Pope Benedict XVI.

GET STARTED

In pairs, on a piece of paper, create two headings. One is the name of your school, the other a different school in your area. In what ways are the schools similar and different? Do you have more in common or more differences?

Develop your knowledge

Major divisions and interpretations

Leaders of different Christian denominations sometimes meet for ecumenical services.

KEY INFORMATION

- There is one Christian family, and all Christians believe that Jesus Christ is their Lord and Saviour. Like all families Christianity has different sections, called denominations.
- The Catholic Church is the biggest single denomination, with over 1 million members around the world. The spiritual leader of the Catholic Church is the Pope (currently Pope Benedict XVI), and the headquarters of the Church is the Vatican, in Rome.
- The origins of the differences between Christians are their different interpretations of important beliefs and values. There are three main traditions in the Christian Churches – the Catholic tradition, the Protestant tradition and the Orthodox tradition.

KEY QUESTIONS

KNOWLEDGE AND UNDERSTANDING

What are the main divisions of the Christian Church?

Why are there different divisions in Christianity?

In what ways is Catholicism different from other Christian denominations?

Is Catholicism practised differently in other parts of the world?

ANALYSIS AND EVALUATION

How important are the divisions in the Church?

Does it matter if different Christians have different beliefs?

- Catholics trace their origins back to the early community of the apostles. Apostolic succession is the key doctrine of Catholic and Orthodox churches; it means that all bishops can show a line of succession all the way back to the apostles. In particular, the Pope is a direct successor to St Peter.
- The Protestant denominations have their roots in the Reformation in 16th-century Germany and England. In Germany, a priest called Martin Luther called for a reform of the Church, based on his concerns about abuses of power and differences of opinion over interpretations of the scriptures. In England, Henry VIII was originally opposed to the ideas of the Reformation, but later saw it as a way of challenging the authority of the Pope to gain a divorce from his wife Catherine of Aragon.
- The Protestant Church has many branches, based on differences in theological interpretations and cultural values. Even within a single branch, there can be very significant differences in points of doctrine.
- The Orthodox tradition is much older than the Protestant. Like the Protestant Church, there are many branches of the Orthodox Church.
- The spread of the three traditions around the world has tended to follow geopolitical lines. Catholicism is predominant in countries with strong links to Italy and Spain (such as most of the countries of South America). Protestantism is common in countries with strong links to Britain, Germany and France, while Orthodox Christianity has been less colonial, and tends to be found in Russian and Eastern European countries.

FOR INTEREST

The **Spanish Inquisition** was set up in 1478 by King Ferdinand II and Queen Isabella I. The aim was to ensure that Catholicism was the religion of the country and required Muslims and Jews to convert or leave. It was finally abolished in 1834. The role of the Grand Inquisitor of the Church is now that of the Head of the Congregation for the Doctrine of the Faith.

KEY WORDS

Anglican A member of the Church of England.

denomination A group within the Christian Church.

ecumenical A movement that brings different churches together.

Eucharist Thanksgiving service celebrating the sacrificial death and resurrection of Jesus Christ; also known as Holy Communion or Mass.

Free Church Non-conformist Church, free from State control.

Lutheran A Protestant Church, named after Martin Luther.

Methodist A Christian who belongs to the Methodist Church, a Free Church founded by John Wesley in the 18th century.

non-conformist Protestant Churches which became separated from the established Church of England in the 17th century.

Orthodox A Church within the Eastern tradition of Christianity. It is also used to mean someone who follows the teaching of their Church (in which case it is written as 'orthodox').

patriarch The title for principal Eastern Orthodox bishops. Also used for early Israelite leaders such as Abraham, Isaac and Jacob.

Pope The Bishop of Rome, head of the Roman Catholic Church.

Protestant (i) The part of the Christian Church which separated from the Roman Catholic and Orthodox Churches in the 16th century when their members professed (or 'protested', hence the name) the centrality of the Bible and other beliefs. (ii) Members of Protestant Churches.

Quaker A member of the Religious Society of Friends, a movement founded in the 17th century by George Fox and which does not fit within the three main traditions of Christianity.

Reformation The historical event that led to the separation of Catholicism from other parts of the Western (not Eastern Orthodox) tradition of Christianity in the 16th century.

Roman Catholic The part of the Church owing loyalty to the Bishop of Rome, as distinct to the Orthodox and Protestant traditions; often abbreviated to 'Catholic'.

schism The technical term used particularly for the split between the Eastern and Western traditions of Christianity in 1054 CE.

Vatican The residence of the Pope in Rome and the administrative centre of the Roman Catholic Church. The main building of the Vatican is St Peter's Basilica, built on the traditional site of St Peter's tomb.

The origins of Catholicism

The next two pages will help you to:

- identify the different traditions within Christianity
- explain the reasons for these different strands.

AO1 skills ACTIVITIES

St Paul refers to the Church as the 'body of Christ'. Draw a large outline of a person. Using newspapers, magazines or drawings fill in the shape with images of people caring for others. Explain how this picture might help a child's understanding of St Paul's words.

The apostolic succession

The roots of Catholicism go right back to the founding of the Church at the time of Jesus. There is an unbroken line which traces its origins to St Peter and the other apostles. This line is used to show the apostolic succession (the direct line from Peter to the present Pope) in disputes over authority within the Church.

FOR INTEREST

'Apostolic succession' is the name the Church uses to demonstrate its claim to authority by pointing to its origins in the work of the apostles. In particular each Pope is shown as a direct successor of St Peter.

The branches of Christianity

John's gospel shows that Jesus himself was aware that there would be different branches of his Church. This is quite normal since human beings will always differ over small details and grow in different directions. It has been estimated that there are over 33,000 different branches, or **denominations**, of Christianity, but they all share the belief that Jesus Christ is the Lord and Saviour of all. All other beliefs, customs and practices are secondary to this one core statement.

John 15:1–4

I am the true vine, and my Father is the vinedresser. Every branch in me that bears no fruit he cuts away, and every branch that does bear fruit he prunes to make it bear even more. You are clean already, by means of the word that I have spoken to you. Remain in me, as I in you. As a branch cannot bear fruit all by itself, unless it remains part of the vine, neither can you unless you remain in me.

Other ways of describing the unity and diversity of Christianity

Idea	Meaning	Origin
Body	This metaphor of the body enables Christians to see the Church as a living organism. Each part of the body has a function to perform which keeps it healthy and efficient. If one part is diseased the others care for it so that the overall effect on the body is reduced. If one bit dies away the whole body suffers and this is to be avoided.	St Paul (1 Corinthians)
Family	Jesus suggested that his community were like brothers and sisters. Each family creates its own identity away from its grandparents or other relatives, though the relationship still exists even if it is in a different form. From time to time families have arguments and disputes but the glue that holds them together, enabling forgiveness and reconciliation, is love.	Jesus in the gospels

Why so many branches?

The technical name for a section of Christianity is a denomination. Many of them were founded as a response to a particular controversy or theological dispute. This is where somebody rejects an item of the Church's teaching and forms a breakaway Church. In one famous example, a theologian called Arius developed a heresy which a majority of Christians at the time (4th century CE) supported. He said that Jesus was created by God and was not himself God. The issue was resolved by a council of the Church and it stayed united – Arian ideas do sometimes reappear throughout the history of Christianity.

Major divisions

The two largest theological disputes which caused splits in the Church, which exist to this day, were the controversy over the *filioque* clause in the creed (see below) and the authority of the Pope, which led to the Protestant Reformation (1517–1648).

The Great Schism of 1054 CE

The Eastern and Western Churches disagreed over a line in the Nicene Creed. Does the Holy Spirit come from God the Father or from both God the Father and Jesus? In the Orthodox Church the words in the Creed are: We believe in the Holy Spirit, the Lord, the giver of life, who proceeds from the Father. The Roman Catholic Church has: We believe in the Holy Spirit, the Lord, the giver of life, who proceeds from the Father and the Son.

This led to the schism between the Western and Eastern sections of Christianity.

AO2 skills ACTIVITIES

One religion; many branches. Examine whether or not the divisions within Christianity are its strength or its downfall. Discuss your thinking with your work partner and add new ideas to your response.

The Roman Catholic tradition

The next two pages will help you to:

- identify the distinctive features of the Roman Catholic tradition
- examine the links between Catholicism and other Christian denominations
- evaluate the relationship between Catholic beliefs and their expression in religious customs or practices.

Catholicism – a global Church

Catholicism is the largest Christian **denomination**. **Roman Catholics** can be found in every country of the world, although there are some places where they make up a much higher proportion of the population, in countries like Ireland, Spain, Italy, Poland and Peru.

The beliefs that Catholics share with other Christians include:

- Jesus Christ is the Lord and Saviour of all
- the Bible is a source of inspiration and wisdom
- there is an afterlife
- Christians should participate in the **Eucharist** in memory of Jesus' actions at the Last Supper.

The beliefs that Catholics hold distinctly from other Christians include:

- the **Pope** is the head of the Church and is the spiritual leader of Christianity
- all priests must remain celibate
- women cannot be admitted to the priesthood.

Some Christians share some of these beliefs with Catholics but disagree in other areas. For example, Anglo-Catholics in the Church of England share all the beliefs of Catholicism but do not accept the primacy of the Bishop of Rome over all other bishops and instead look to the Archbishop of Canterbury as their spiritual leader.

Matthew 16:17–19

Jesus replied, 'Simon son of Jonah, you are a blessed man! Because it was no human agency that revealed this to you but my Father in heaven. So I now say to you: You are Peter and on this rock I will build my community. And the gates of the underworld can never overpower it. I will give you the keys of the kingdom of Heaven: whatever you bind on earth will be bound in heaven; whatever you loose on earth will be loosed in heaven.'

AO1 skills ACTIVITIES

Create a spider diagram with the words 'Christian Church' in the middle. On your page identify the key beliefs and practices of the Christian religion. Underline the ones which are followed by Catholics.

Catholics celebrating mass in Peru.

Movements within the Catholic Church

One of the great strengths of Catholicism until the second half of the 20th century was that it looked much the same wherever it was found. The unifying factor was the language of Latin. All services and prayers were written and said in Latin, and hymns were sung in Latin. Since the Second **Vatican** Council (1962–65), Catholic Churches have been able to use the language of their own country for services, prayers and hymns, and the Bible. This has been accompanied with an opening-up of the Church, which has led to a much greater diversity in Catholic practice and customs. It has also led to the development of new branches of the Church.

Charismatic renewal

In the 1960s, there was a spiritual revival among Catholics, which reflected the culture of Western society at the time. It was associated with the 'hippy' movement and concentration on personal religious journeys and quests. Free expression meant that Catholics could worship their God however they chose. Many believed that the Holy Spirit could be called upon to intervene in the course of history and shifted their emphasis away from Eucharistic practices towards more charismatic practices, which were contained in prayer meetings. These meetings were often spontaneous, accompanied by contemporary music and dance, had little structure and were joyful.

Opus Dei

The organisation Opus Dei (meaning 'The Work of God') believes that the Church is at its strongest when it is tightly controlled, where it has a clear sense of purpose, where its doctrines are well known and understood and where it stands as counter to the prevailing secular culture.

Founded in the middle of the last century by a Spanish priest called Josemaría Escrivá, Opus Dei is an organisation of the Church which sits outside normal diocesan controls and is committed to the maintenance of traditional Catholic values and practices. It is associated with strong moral principles, especially in relation to family life. Opus Dei has been the subject of much criticism from Catholics and others.

REMEMBER THIS

'Secular' is the word that is used to describe everything that is non-religious. Secular culture is that which pays no attention to the religious or spiritual values of society. When Christian groups react against this, they are continuing a long-held tradition established by Jesus in his criticism of the ways of the Pharisees and their associates.

AO2 skills ACTIVITIES

Imagine you are a reporter who is assigned to interview the Pope. Identify what questions you would like to ask him. In small groups share your ideas and compile a Top Ten list of questions which you think would be of importance to young Catholics today to know and understand. If time allows choose one to answer yourselves from the Pope's point of view.

The Orthodox tradition

The next two pages will help you to:

- examine the differences between the Catholic and the Orthodox traditions.

The Serbian Orthodox church of Saint Sava in Belgrade, Serbia.

One Pope or many patriarchs?

In the early days of Christianity, not long after the death of Jesus, there were five main centres of Christianity, each with its own spiritual leader: Jerusalem, Rome, Antioch (in modern Turkey), Alexandria (in Egypt) and Byzantium. Byzantium became Constantinople, named after the famous Roman emperor Constantine and is known today as Istanbul. It is located at the entrance to the Bosphorus and has been a strategically important city throughout its history. The **Patriarch** of Constantinople was an important overseer (bishop) of the Church, comparable in influence to the Bishop of Rome.

AO1 skills ACTIVITIES

Describe five common but distinctive features of belief and practice in the Orthodox tradition. Draw an outline of three people kneeling, sitting or standing in prayer. Underneath each picture suggest the possible advantages of each position.

Constantine's contribution to Christianity was enormous. It was his Edict of Milan in 313 CE that made Christianity the official religion of the Roman Empire. This is significant because the outbreak of a theological argument between scholars in the East and West developed into a battle of wills between the head of the Church in Rome – the **Pope** – and the head of the Church in the east – the Patriarch of Constantinople. This led to the Great **Schism** of 1054 CE, which centred around what is known as the *filioque* clause of the Nicene Creed (see Topic 3.1).

1054 CE: The Great Schism. The Eastern and Western Churches disagreed over a line in the Nicene Creed. Does the Holy Spirit come from God the Father or from both God the Father and Jesus? In the Orthodox Church the words in the Creed are: We believe in the Holy Spirit, the Lord, the giver of life, who proceeds from the Father through the Son (*per filio*). The Roman Catholic Church has: We believe in the Holy Spirit, the Lord, the giver of life, who proceeds from the Father and the Son (*filioque*)

Key differences between the Catholic and Orthodox traditions

In addition to the *filioque* clause, there are other important differences between the **Catholic** and **Orthodox** traditions:

- Orthodox worship is usually in Greek, not in Latin
- Orthodox worship includes the veneration of icons and the screening of the high altar in churches by use of an iconostasis (a screen of icons)
- decision making and authority are vested in the Patriarch of Constantinople, not the Pope.

Worship in the Orthodox tradition

Catholic worship, except in the charismatic renewal services (see Topic 3.2), is usually fixed, so that the audience can participate fully in the sacrament of the Mass. In contrast, Orthodox worship takes much longer, and most of its actions are carried out by the priest or his attendants. The congregation come and go as they please. Much of the activity occurs behind the iconostasis, creating a sense of mystery, as if the priest were enacting the eternal banquet that all will experience when they get to heaven. The role of the people is to contemplate this spectacle and pray to share in it when the time comes.

The idea of the eternal banquet in heaven is found in this parable in Matthew's gospel:

Matthew 22:8–10

Then he said to his servants, 'The wedding is ready; but as those who were invited proved to be unworthy, go to the main crossroads and invite everyone you can find to come to the wedding.' So these servants went out onto the roads and collected together everyone they could find, bad and good alike; and the wedding hall was filled with guests.

REMEMBER THIS

It is important to note that there are many branches of the Orthodox tradition; it is not a unified **denomination** in its own right. Local variations often reflect national boundaries, ethnic or cultural considerations or historical differences. Among other Orthodox traditions are the Russian, Coptic (Egyptian), Armenian, Serbian and Greek churches, each with its own distinct style.

MUST THINK ABOUT!

The average length of a Russian Orthodox liturgy is four hours. Russian Orthodox churches have no seats or benches so the congregation stands to watch the sacred liturgy. People come and go while the Mass is in progress. The clergy read from the scriptures, preach about them and celebrate the Eucharist while there is constant movement.

AO1 skills ACTIVITIES

Research and explore the reasons why the Orthodox Church emphasises the mystery of God in their worship and their buildings. Compare and contrast this with the Catholic tradition. Most Orthodox families celebrate their own saint's day with special customs and practices. Examine the importance of this tradition and explore how keeping these days might encourage the faith, especially in the younger members of the family.

The Protestant Reformation

The next two pages will help you to:

- explain the differences between the Catholic and Protestant traditions
- identify the differences between denominations within the Protestant tradition.

Martin Luther

In 1517 CE Martin Luther, a German Augustinian priest, nailed a document to the door of Wittenburg Cathedral. That act marks the symbolic beginning of the **Reformation**. The document contained 95 theses (statements) about what was wrong with the Church at that stage of the 16th century. It is symbolic because the document was a summary of many years of growing concern and theological disagreements that Luther had with the Church. Luther believed that:

- the Church should allow the Bible to be translated from Latin into the vernacular so that all people could understand it in their own language
- the practices of selling indulgences should be abolished
- the **Pope** exploited his position and abused his power and should be restricted in what he could do
- the teaching of the Church should be based on scripture alone
- the way to salvation was by faith alone – people could not buy their way into heaven by good works, however good or charitable they might be
- relics of the saints should be used as aids to prayer, and should not be sold to collect money for the Church.

AO1 skills ACTIVITIES

Briefly describe how and explain why the Reformation occurred. If it had not started with Martin Luther, do you think the Reformation would have eventually happened anyway? Why?

Reactions to Luther

In England, there were people who were strongly opposed to the Reformation as well as those who supported it wholeheartedly. The monarch of England held the post of Defender of the Faith (or *Fidei Defensor* in Latin – you can see these letters on the engravings on British coins), and was supposed to uphold the Catholic faith. At that time, the monarch was King Henry VIII, and he was initially opposed to the ideas of the Reformation, although he later changed his mind (see Topic 3.5).

On the other side, people who shared Luther's ideas in England included William Tyndale, who tried to translate the Bible into English. Other supporters in Europe included John Calvin, a French reformer whose ideas culminated in building a Protestant community in Geneva in Switzerland, and Ulrich Zwingli, who was active as a reformer in Switzerland. Each of these caused a new Church to be founded, and each new Church had its own unique interpretation of the Christian message.

In 1517 CE Martin Luther nailed his 95 Theses to the door of Wittenburg Cathedral.

FOR INTEREST

At the time of Martin Luther, it was common for pardoners to travel the Holy Roman Empire, gathering money by selling 'indulgences' (see Chaucer's 'The Pardoner's Tale'). These were a bond between the Church and the purchaser which promised them a quicker route into Heaven. It was a way of buying back punishments for the sins that a person had committed.

The Holy Roman Empire was a union of countries in central Europe, which began around 962 and ended in 1806. The first Holy Roman Emperor was Otto the Great and the last Francis II. There was often tension between the Holy Roman Empire and the Papacy.

Protestant worship

In simplistic terms, many **Protestant** Churches tend to put greater emphasis on ministry of the Word. That is why the central architectural feature of many Protestant churches will be the pulpit, from which the vicar or priest will deliver the sermon. The sermon will be a central part of Sunday worship, and the ministers of these Churches are usually very learned people. Their ceremonial dress will comprise academic gowns as a sign of their learning.

The Anglican Reformation

The next two pages will help you to:

- explain the differences between the Protestant Reformation and the Anglican Reformation
- explain the underlying reasons for the Anglican Reformation.

In the Anglican Church, women can become priests.

AO1 skills ACTIVITIES

Briefly describe how and explain why the Church of England developed from the Protestant Reformation. Make a list of all the places around the globe where Anglicanism is practised. Identify what they have in common.

Henry VIII and the Church

The origins of the **Anglican Reformation** are found in the **Protestant** Reformation. Although Henry VIII reacted aggressively to Luther and Tyndale's arguments for the Reformation, he had his own confrontation with the **Pope** when he tried to divorce Catherine of Aragon. Recognising that the reformers were challenging the authority of the Pope, Henry saw a way of getting what he wanted. The outcome was the Church of England.

Anglo-Catholics

There are some churches in England that are barely distinguishable from **Roman Catholic** churches. They have celibate priests; they have Mass, Benediction and Stations of the Cross; they celebrate all the major Catholic feasts. The only difference is that in matters of faith and morals, they look to the Archbishop of Canterbury for judgement, accepting that the Pope has a special place in Christendom, even if he does not have authority over them.

Anglican Protestants

Some Churches of England, at the other end of the spectrum, organise themselves and their belief system much more in keeping with **Lutheran** principles. Some choose to call themselves evangelicals and emphasise the priority of Biblical principles over Church doctrines. While Anglo-Catholic parishes will have very traditional worship, based on the Catholic Missal (the book containing all the prayers and responses needed to celebrate Mass), Anglican Protestants are more likely to use *Common Worship*, published in 2001 CE.

Anglicanism – a broad church

The style of worship and the approach to faith and morals in any particular church is likely to reflect the particular beliefs of the local vicar. Country vicars are often called rectors and may well look after two or three parishes. Local clergy (vicar, rector or curate – assistant priest) will usually be appointed by the local bishop. The appointments are often said to be made to the 'living' – it is called this because, in the past, the parish had to fund the living costs of the priest and her or his family.

Differences between Anglicanism and Catholicism

In general terms, the differences between Anglicans and Catholics are:

- women are allowed in the priesthood in the Anglican Church
- clergy are allowed to get married in the Anglican Church
- in certain circumstances, people who have been divorced can be re-admitted to the sacraments in the Anglican Church
- Anglicans do not accept the authority of the Pope.

Anglicanism – a global community

There are some important world leaders who are Anglicans. The Queen is an Anglican and so is Archbishop Desmond Tutu, the South African human rights activist. They are united by their being in full communion with the Anglican Church whose spiritual home is Canterbury in Kent.

In England, the Church of England is the 'established' Church. This means that it should operate in harmony with the political system. The Queen is the head of the Church, a position established by Henry VIII. It also means that when people are asked what religion they are, they are likely to say they are Church of England. A person who says this on entering a hospital may well receive a visit from an Anglican chaplain.

MUST THINK ABOUT!

Your experience of Anglican Churches is most likely to be the Church of England, but it has counterparts in Wales (Church of Wales), Scotland (Church of Scotland) Ireland (Church of Ireland) and so on. In other countries, those who are in full communion with the Church of England may be called Episcopalian Churches on the basis of being run by Bishops.

AO2 skills ACTIVITIES

Explore the idea that the Church of England grew out of a political dispute for power rather than a religious disagreement over belief and practice. How much do you think it matters why the Reformation occurred?

Examine the idea that the Anglican Church is just an English version of the Catholic Church, but without the Pope at its head. What arguments could you put forward to support or deny this view?

Interpreting practice

The next two pages will help you to:

- explain the differences in practice within the Catholic Church
- explore the reasons why some Catholics believe different things
- evaluate at least one difference in practice within Catholicism.

A Catholic receives communion at the Mass.

Different responses to the Eucharist

Some **Catholics** will only receive communion directly from the priest. They may also prefer to receive the host (consecrated wafer) direct to their tongue and not into their hand. Such people often kneel to receive the host and may not take communion in the form of wine.

There are many others who prefer to participate in communion by sharing wine from a chalice and a piece of bread torn off one loaf. Communion celebrated in this way may take place in a house or an open space and will be very informal (see also Topic 4).

Different responses to prayer

Although there is just one Catholic tradition, there is scope for great diversity in the Church. If you visit a Catholic church around noon on the first Friday of every month, it is likely that you will find a small group of its parishioners taking part in Benediction, saying the rosary or praying a novena. These are formal prayers which play an important part of the life of some Catholics.

AO1 skills ACTIVITIES

With your work partner choose a game and outline its rules. Discuss whether or not it matters if others change or ignore the rules of the game. Give reasons for your answers.

However, there are other parishes (or even other churches in the same parish) where groups of Catholics meet informally, perhaps in each other's houses or in the open air. They may pray spontaneously, putting into their own words the things they want God to know about. They may chant quietly, especially if they have been influenced by the community at Taizé in France. Alternatively they may just sit in silence contemplating something, someone or the words of a reading. Prayer that is spoken from the heart is called 'extempore' prayer.

Music in the liturgy

Nowhere is there greater diversity in Catholicism than in the use of music for the Mass. There are some Catholics who prefer their worship to be quiet and solemn and are quite happy if there is no music at all. Many traditional Catholics prefer the meditative beauty created by the singing of plain chant often associated with monastic communities.

Most Catholics are familiar with the 'hymn sandwich' approach, where hymns are chosen that match the liturgical season or the theme of the liturgy. There are even some parishes which have adopted **Free Church** worship styles, where a worship band leads the singing with whichever instruments are available at the time. This is in contrast to the solo organ that commonly accompanies hymn singing in most parishes.

Different responses to initiation into the Church

One area in which Catholicism differs significantly from some other **denominations** is in the sacrament of confirmation. Confirmation is an initiation rite in Catholic and **Protestant** Churches which confirms a person as a full member of the Church.

The difference between Catholicism and most other denominations comes from the difference between them over the practice of infant baptism. In many Protestant Churches, a baptised child does not become a full member of the Church, and full membership only comes with confirmation, usually when the child is in their early teens.

In the Catholic Church, a child does become a full member of the Church when they are baptised. According to the catechism, the sacrament of confirmation 'renders our bond with the Church more perfect'. For an adult joining the Church, baptism and confirmation occur simultaneously and are followed by their first Holy Communion. If, as is common, an infant is baptised and the child then makes their first communion around the age of seven, it is usual for them to be confirmed in their teenage years. However, many Catholic dioceses are now confirming children before they receive Holy Communion. They would generally say that taking Holy Communion is about being in full communion with the Church. Many young Catholics never make this step because they become alienated from the Church before they get to the point where confirmation is available to them.

RESEARCH NOTE

The Latin Mass Society is an organisation committed to retaining the traditional Latin Catholic Mass. They publicise those places where such a Mass is to be said and they provide a network for those people who would not like the old customs to die out. There are many older Catholics who can remember a time when every Mass was said in Latin. You can read more about this on the Latin Mass Society website.

FOR DEBATE

'An electric guitar is hardly the way to create an appropriate atmosphere of worship in a church.' What do you think of this statement? Discuss this with your work partner.

AO2 skills ACTIVITIES

St Paul wrote that all people who are baptised into the one Spirit are all one in Christ Jesus. Examine whether this teaching supports or rejects the different ways in which the Eucharist is celebrated.

Create your own religion. It needs to include, among other features, a name, a past history, a holy book, a set of beliefs and a code of practice. Share your new religion with the rest of the class.

Cultural diversity within Catholicism

The next two pages will help you to:

- identify some of the different cultural expressions of Catholicism
- explain the reasons for cultural diversity within Catholicism
- evaluate the strengths and weaknesses of cultural diversity within the Catholic religious tradition.

The Black Madonna of Częstochowa in Poland.

AO1 skills **ACTIVITIES**

Working in pairs think of a national organisation with many branches or services up and down the country. Make a list of the advantages of being centrally governed and organised.

Case study 1: Polish Catholics

During the Second World War many Polish soldiers came to Britain to fight against the German forces that had conquered their country. They brought their **Catholic** faith with them. Many stayed on and it is quite common for parishes, especially those in big cities, to have at least one Mass in Polish on a Sunday. The opening up of the European Union has also resulted in the more recent arrival of many Polish people and other Eastern Europeans.

Polish Catholics have a strong sense of devotion to Our Lady of Częstochowa – or the Black Madonna as she is known. This is a famous painting of Mary and Jesus in a similar style to an Eastern icon.

Young Polish Catholics are often seen at church in their scout uniform. This is because scouting is seen, by Poles, as a way of serving God and your country.

Case study 2: West Indian Catholics

The Catholicism that is to be found in the West Indies is very different from British and Polish Catholicism. West Indian Catholicism arrived in Britain through immigration, particularly in the 1950s and 1960s. Worship often reflects the cultural style of Caribbean Catholics so it may be accompanied by steel drums, calypso or reggae-inspired music. Dancing and singing may also feature in the worship.

Acts of the Apostles 2:7–12

They were amazed and astonished. 'Surely,' they said, 'all these men speaking are Galileans? How does it happen that each of us hears them in his own native language? Parthians, Medes and Elamites; people from Mesopotamia, Judaea and Cappadocia, Pontus and Asia, Phrygia and Pamphylia, Egypt and the parts of Libya round Cyrene; residents of Rome – Jews and proselytes alike – Cretans and Arabs, we hear them preaching in our own language about the marvels of God.' Everyone was amazed and perplexed; they asked one another what it all meant.

Case study 3: Asian Catholics

If you were to travel to India, China, Japan or other Asian countries and go into Catholic churches, you would see images of Jesus that resembled local men. Since no one can be sure what Jesus looked like it is not surprising that there are many images to choose from.

The Tamil community from India has a very strong identity, which stems from the tradition that the apostle Thomas went to Tamil Nadu around 50 CE and was martyred there. Some of the practices of Tamil Christians reflect the local customs and religious practices of their local Hindu neighbours. The wearing of flowers and the adorning of statues with them is a custom associated with these Asian Catholics but is different from the ways in which Western Catholics worship.

RESEARCH NOTE

Using the Internet and an atlas, try to find the countries named in the passage cited from the Acts of the Apostles. Work out how far away from Israel these places are and work out: how many continents are covered; how many languages may have been spoken; and how easy it would have been to visit each one on a regular basis before cars were invented. Then ask yourself if it is any wonder there is diversity within the Church.

AO2 skills ACTIVITIES

Throughout Great Britain, Catholic migrants from other nationalities are filling the churches. Choose one example and consider the positive impact of their presence on Church practice today.

In pairs or a small group, devise an assembly which includes expressions of worship used by Catholics around the world. The prayers, music and dance should reflect the different customs and concerns of the people. Explain your choices.

The Free Churches

The next two pages will help you to:

- explore the reasons for the different Free Church denominations
- explain the differences between the Free Church traditions.

A Methodist Church in the United States of America.

The aftermath of the Reformation

The history of humanity contains many examples of major upheavals which result in a period of instability. In recent history the tearing down of the Berlin Wall started a widespread change across Europe, the ripples from which are still felt today. It was the same with the **Reformation**. Luther's action prompted a tidal wave of change through Christianity and the result was a series of smaller Churches, each with their own particular identity. Among these are the **Free Churches**. The Free Churches are so-called because they became free of institutional or political control.

AO1 skills ACTIVITIES

Make three columns in your book with the headings 'Catholic' 'Protestant' and 'Non-conformist'. In each column list the distinctive features and practices of each Church. What conclusions could you draw about the Christian religion from these three different traditions?

Methodism

A good example of a Free Church is the **Methodist** Church. The Methodist Church has its origins in the life and work of John Wesley (1703–91), an **Anglican** clergyman in 18th-century England. The Methodist movement used a methodical approach to Bible study and scriptures as a way of guiding Christian living. Wesley was particularly active in preaching to the working classes, often in large open-air services. It is said that he preached more than 40,000 times in his lifetime, travelling 250,000 miles on horseback.

Wesley wanted to make the message of Jesus relevant to 18th-century working class communities. Some of the unique features of Methodism which help to show how it is different from Catholicism are:

- the strong sense of small 'class' study and prayer – people met in the homes of fellow Methodists
- the strong emphasis on a work ethic which requires Methodists to give a good day's service for a fair wage
- an emphasis on temperance – alcohol was considered such a problem for the working classes that it was discouraged among Methodists. Non-alcoholic grape juice is used in communion to avoid the charge of hypocrisy.

Non-conformity

'Non-conformity' is the term applied to Christians who break away from institutional control and do not want to conform to the dominance of the Church. Many of the early **Non-conformists** followed the theological principles of the more extreme reformers who were not satisfied with the simple removal of the authority of the **Pope**. They wanted control over their own congregations, their worship and their Church's organisation. Some of the things that distinguish Non-conformists from **Catholics** are:

- emphasis on the decision-making powers of the elders of the Church
- selection of ministers by the congregation, not bishops
- more open and free styles of worship
- emphasis on the study of the scriptures and the Christian life through Sunday Schools where the children are educated separately from the adults.

Some Free Churches that might be present in the local community are:

- the Salvation Army
- the Plymouth Brethren
- the Religious Society of Friends (the **Quakers**)
- the Anabaptists.

MUST THINK ABOUT!

Many of the Free Churches support what is called the **'Protestant** work ethic'. They believe that God gave each person skills, gifts and talents to put to good use and that it is only fair and reasonable to give him thanks and praise by putting these skills and talents to good use. If an employer has provided a person with the means to support herself or himself and their family, it is morally praiseworthy for that person to work hard. 'The Devil makes work for idle hands' is a well-known phrase that indicates what might happen if someone is not employed doing productive activities.

FOR DEBATE

The United States of America is known as the 'Land of the brave and home of the free'. This is because many of the early European settlers were fleeing from religious persecution at home. Set up a class debate that explores the statement: 'Being religious is about being free to believe what you want.'

AO2 skills ACTIVITIES

The Free Churches were made up of Christians who felt dissatisfied with the Protestant tradition. Examine the reasons for their dissatisfaction and the appropriateness of the name they were given.

Some Non-conformist groups prefer to minister to the people on the streets rather than wait for them to come to their church, for example the Salvation Army. Explore the strengths and weaknesses of this approach.

Churches working together

The next two pages will help you to:

- explore the organisation and practices of ecumenism
- explore the work of the World Council of Churches
- evaluate whether differences between **denominations** can or should be resolved.

Ecumenism

Ecumenical is derived from the Greek word *oikoumene* which means 'of the inhabited earth'. The Ecumenical movement aims to bring all Churches together in unity, remembering that they are all followers of Jesus and worship the same God. Supporters of ecumenism argue that Jesus would never have wanted Christians to argue among themselves and divide into different denominations.

1 Corinthians 12:27

Now you are the body of Christ, and each one of you is a part of it.

Matthew 22:39b

Love your neighbour as yourself.

Important developments in the history of Ecumenicism include:

- 1910: Edinburgh, Scotland: Churches discuss how they can work together in foreign countries. Can missionaries working for different Churches stop competing for converts and share resources and buildings?
- 1927: Lausanne, Switzerland: A multi-denominational conference to discuss differences between different denominations.
- 1948: The World Council of Churches was formed after the Second World War (1939–45). Every member must accept the Christian belief that Jesus Christ is God and Saviour of the world and that Christians are 'All one in Christ'.

If Christians from around the world and from different denominations can talk together and discuss their differences why can't countries? If Christians can work together to encourage peace and justice by helping others in need, it would set a good example for everyone else to follow. Christian Aid is the aid agency of World Council of Churches.

Initially, 148 **Protestant** Churches joined the Council. Since then, more Protestant denominations have joined. The **Orthodox** Church joined in 1961 and, although the Roman **Catholic** Church has not officially joined, it sends official observers. The Council aims to meet every eight years.

AO1 skills ACTIVITIES

Scenario: A member of your class is trying to organise a class trip to the cinema with a meal but is having trouble deciding where to eat and what film to watch so that everyone will come. Was it easy to reach agreement? Did you have to compromise? Is everyone going to attend? Why or why not? Would your differences stop you from being friends? What are the possible solutions?

AO1 skills ACTIVITIES

Local churches would like a logo to use that symbolises the work that they are trying to do in bringing church communities together. Design a logo that demonstrates their commitment to **Ecumenical** practice but also their individuality.

Some topics that have been discussed at the World Council of Churches include:

- Theological differences between different Churches, for example what actually happens at the Eucharist? Is it a reminder of Jesus' death and sacrifice or does it transubstantiate into Jesus' body and blood?
- What makes a person a Christian? Is it baptism? Living a Christian life? Personal repentance and asking for your sins to be forgiven? A combination of these?
- War (is it right for Christians to fight?), racism, homosexuality and poverty.

The logo of the World Council of Churches.

How does ecumenism work in Britain?

Once denominations start talking to each other, some of them find they have many things in common and that they can compromise where they have differences and so they decide to unite. So far this has been among smaller denominations; for example, the Presbyterian and Congregational denominations became the United Reformed Church in 1972. There have also been discussions about the Methodist Church reuniting with the Church of England (remember it began because of disagreements with the Church of England back in the 18th century).

Most ecumenical work takes place between individual Christians who are either friends who attend different churches, or Christians who live locally and are concerned by something happening in their local area.

Other denominations

- 'Churches Together in Britain and Ireland' acts as a central point for any churches wishing to work together – the offices, staff and website share examples of good practice and offer advice.
- 'Churches for All' (CfA) helps churches to become disability friendly. How can churches best adapt buildings for wheelchairs, blind or partially sighted people and the hard of hearing? How can churches involve physically and mentally disabled people in youth groups, musical groups, etc.?
- 'More Than Gold' encourages churches to work together to serve sport and the community. Its aim is to involve Christians in London's 2012 Olympics. It wants churches to offer hospitality for athletes' families, to provide chaplains to the Olympic village and to offer care and refreshments for spectators.

RESEARCH NOTE

Contact your local churches and find out how they work together.

Shared churches and worship

Different churches are sharing buildings and holding joint services either because the number of people attending church has fallen or because new housing estates are being built and Christians want to have a presence there. This means sharing a building and a minister.

Two churches that have joined together in one building are St Andrew's Shared Church in Cippenham, Slough. Here Anglicans and Catholics share a building and have common activities, but have also kept distinct services and groups.

AO2 skills ACTIVITIES

Imagine you are on an ecumenical working party that has the task of drawing up plans for an ecumenical church for a new housing estate. The following denominations have agreed to share a building and a youth worker: Church of England, Pentecostal and Roman Catholic. Consider the ways that these denominations can work together and the practicalities involved. Your plans must give detailed reasons for your choices and explain where it was difficult to reach consensus.

Ecumenical communities: Taizé, Iona and Corrymeela

The next two pages will help you to:

- explore the practices of the Taizé, Iona and Corrymeela communities
- explain why these communities are important to some Catholics
- evaluate the advantages and disadvantages of visiting ecumenical communities.

Taizé

In 1940 Roger Schutz founded a religious community of monks at Taizé in France that sheltered Jewish refugees escaping Nazi Germany until 1942. When the Nazis occupied France, Roger had to leave but returned at the end of the war, initially caring for German prisoners of war, practising the Christian belief of forgiveness and reconciliation.

Taizé is a place of pilgrimage particularly for young people from all over the world and, as an **ecumenical** community, works to break down barriers between Christian **denominations**. The monks also are from different Churches and different countries.

Young people camp in the fields, join in daily worship and help with practical work in the kitchens and on the farms. Worship includes simple songs in Latin, French, German and English. There is time for meditation and reflection, allowing young people to develop self-awareness of what is in their heart and to listen to God. Times of group discussion encourage listening skills and provide a chance to discuss the challenges of being a young Christian. Living a simpler monastic life without television and luxuries helps people find a meaning to life and to decide what is really important.

Iona

The island is situated off the coast of Scotland and has a long history as a religious centre and place of pilgrimage. In 563 St Columba came to Iona with a group of monks hoping to convert local people to Christianity. The monastery was rebuilt in the 1930s by the Reverend George Macleod and a group of unemployed people from Glasgow. Having experienced the benefits of living in a community Reverend Macleod hoped they would return home and encourage a community spirit and way of life in their city and neighbourhood.

Today Iona is a place where ministers and ordinary Christians come to spend a week living simply, spending time in prayer and reading the Bible. They can also reflect on how they spend their time and money and meet together to share their experiences of living as a Christian.

It is also an opportunity to discuss some of the problem areas and issues facing the world and to work out how a Christian should respond to these problems. Recent issues have included global poverty and injustice, the environment and immigration.

RESEARCH NOTE

Taizé is a place visited primarily by young people and some have recorded their experiences on YouTube and on the Taizé website. View some of their video entries and record your impressions of Taizé and reflect on why it is so popular with young people.

MUST THINK ABOUT!

If there was an issue in the world today that the Iona community ought to be considering, what would it be and why?

AO1 skills ACTIVITIES

How would your neighbourhood or town change if people practised a community spirit?

St Mary's Abbey, Iona.

Corrymeela

"If Christianity has nothing to say about reconciliation, then it has nothing to say."

These are the words of the founder of Corrymeela, Reverend Dr R.R. Davey. Corrymeela was established to provide an opportunity for reconciliation and developing understanding among people in Northern Ireland. When it was set up it was unique in Ireland.

Stephen (a **Protestant**) has been to stay at Corrymeela several times and had this to say about his experience.

"Although Northern Ireland is peaceful now, before the Good Friday agreement in 1998 there was always the risk of a terrorist shooting or bomb by the IRA (who wanted a United Ireland) or by the UDA/UDF (who wanted Northern Ireland to stay part of the UK). Protestants and Catholics did not mix – we went to separate schools, had no friends who were Catholic, hardly anyone married a Catholic and we lived in different parts of Belfast. The first time I went [to Corrymeela] my school took us. We met pupils from Catholic schools and realised we weren't that different! I've been back several times now because it is still great to have time in a beautiful place to talk to people you wouldn't otherwise meet. Last time I went it was for a weekend on Third World Development and I met people from other countries. It opens your horizons."

AO2 skills ACTIVITIES

Make a list of all the advantages of visiting an ecumenical community such as Taizé. What are the disadvantages of visiting an ecumenical community instead of your local church?

GradeStudio

Welcome to the Grade Studio

GCSE is about what you can do, not what you can't do. You need to know what examiners want in your answers so that you can get the best possible marks. See pages 30 and 31 for a fuller explanation of the Grade Studio and assessment objectives.

AO1

Question

Explain why Catholics and one other Christian denomination worship in different ways. **[6 marks]**

This question is asking for the reasons for differences in worship. One way to approach this is to refer to the history of the two denominations that leads to the differences in authority and practice. You could build a response in this way:

Student's answer

Catholics and Protestant Christians worship in different ways because they believe different things are important. For example, Catholics believe that only men can be priests and their services are led by men, but Protestants believe that their ministers can be either men or women and their services are led by either.

Examiner's comment

This candidate has written an adequate answer. It gives a simple statement about how the differences in ways of worship can be explained because their worship and practices have developed along different lines. It shows the student is aware of one area of difference between two denominations but lacks the knowledge and background of the divisions (Level 1).

Student's improved answer

Roman Catholics differ from other denominations because they look to the Church and the Pope for spiritual leadership as much as they do to the Bible. In 1054 the Great Schism occurred, dividing the East and the West. The Orthodox Church broke away from the rule of the Pope. Later, during the Reformation, the Protestants broke away again. This resulted in Christians emphasising different parts of their beliefs and organising their services and church buildings in different ways. For instance, the Catholic services are allowed to be said in the country's language, but this is not the case for the Orthodox Church. Catholics use statues and the saying of the rosary to help them pray, but Orthodox Christians prefer the use of icons.

Examiner's comment

The candidate has written a good answer because they have included accurate knowledge, the correct religious terminology and have given several examples to explain their point. The relevant examples are Roman Catholic worship being conducted in the local language, that contrasts with the use of ancient liturgy by Orthodox Christians, the use of icons by Orthodox Christians whilst Roman Catholics prefer other artefacts such as statues and the rosary (Level 3).

AO2

Question

Evaluate the statement: 'Differences between Christians show the faith to be weak.' **[12 marks]**

Student's answer

Christians do not agree on many issues and spend most of the time trying to out-do each other, which makes them weak.

Examiner's comment

The candidate has made a clear statement but it lacks a context, example or consequence (Level 1).

Student's answer

Christians do not agree on many issues concerning faith and practice, such as women priests and remarriage in a church. In the past, these differences have led to wars between Christians, for example in Northern Ireland, and made the Church seem weak and divided.

Examiner's comment

This candidate has given a satisfactory response because they have included examples and have shown how the differences between the denominations can have a negative impact (Level 2).

Student's improved answer

All Christians believe in the central parts of their faith, for instance that Jesus was the Son of God and that he rose from the dead. However, they differ among themselves over some beliefs and practices, such as the importance of Mary and going on pilgrimages. This weakens the Church when Christians resort to fighting over these matters. It can lead to discrimination and violence and even war, as in Northern Ireland. It makes outsiders think religion is not worth bothering about and can confuse young believers. On the other hand, the differences can be a sign of strength. They offer choice, stimulate debate and allow for change and growth. Personally, I think that differences weaken the Church because Jesus started one Church and wanted people to be one.

Examiner's comment

This candidate has written a very good response. There is evidence, examples, two valid points of view and a personal response (Level 4).

These specimen answers provide an outline of how you could construct your response. Space does not allow us to give a full response. The examiner will be looking for more detail in your actual exam responses.

Remember and Reflect

AO1 Describe, explain and analyse, using knowledge and understanding

	Find the answer on:
1 What does the word denomination mean? Give three examples of Christian denominations.	PAGE 65
2 What do the following words mean? a *Catholic* b *Orthodox* c *Protestant*	PAGE 65
3 What was the split between the Roman Catholic Church and Orthodox Church called?	PAGE 67
4 What is meant by the word 'schism'?	PAGE 67
5 List five other denominations of Christianity that you are likely to encounter in England.	PAGE 65
6 Describe the role played by Henry VIII in the Reformation.	PAGE 74
7 Describe the role played by the Pope in the Reformation.	PAGE 74
8 What contribution did Martin Luther make to the Reformation?	PAGE 72
9 What is a Protestant?	PAGE 65
10 Can you be a Protestant and a member of the Church of England? Explain your answer, giving reasons.	PAGE 75
11 Why is the Queen of England the head of the Church of England?	PAGE 75
12 What does the word 'ecumenical' mean?	PAGE 82
13 Explain the aims of the World Council of Churches.	PAGE 82
14 Explain three ways in which different Christian denominations and Churches are working together in Britain.	PAGE 83
15 Name an ecumenical community and explain why it started and what it aims are.	PAGE 84
16 What is a Free Church? In your answer refer to the theological reasons why some Churches are called 'free'.	PAGE 80
17 Who was Josemaría Escrivá? What was his contribution to the development of Catholicism?	PAGE 69
18 Explain what is meant by the term 'Charismatic renewal'.	PAGE 69
19 Name four differences between the Catholic Church and the Orthodox Churches of the Eastern tradition.	PAGE 71

AO2 Use evidence and reasoned argument to express and evaluate personal responses, informed insights, and differing viewpoints

1. The best-known Christian in England is probably the Archbishop of Canterbury, currently Dr Rowan Williams. For many years Canterbury was the centre of the Christian faith in England. Why don't English Catholics recognise the Archbishop of Canterbury as their spiritual leader any longer? What do you think of this?
2. How important were the causes of the Schism between the Church of Rome (Catholicism) and the Orthodox Churches of the Eastern tradition?
3. How important were the causes of the Reformation which caused the split between the Church of Rome (Catholicism) and other Churches in the Western tradition?
4. To what extent do you think it is important that the members of the Catholic Church all believe the same thing? Which is more important: uniformity of belief or the tolerance and acceptance of alternative points of view? Give reasons for your answer.
5. 'The great thing about the Latin Mass was that wherever you were in the world, you always knew what was going on.' How true do you think this statement is? Would you prefer the words of the Mass to be spoken in a universal language or in one that was local to the worshipping community? Explain why you think what you do.
6. 'One bread, one body, one Lord of all.' To what extent is this quotation from St Paul a fair reflection of the state of the Church at the present time?
7. Catholics believe that the Pope acts as a bridge between them and God (*pontifex*). Do you need a go-between in your relationship with God? Even if you have no relationship with God, explain why you think some people do need a go-between. Give reasons for your argument and show your thinking.
8. 'The Churches should set aside their differences and join together under one leader.' How far would you agree with this statement? How might Catholics respond to it?
9. 'If Christians can't even agree about the Eucharist then there is no hope of unity between the Churches.' Give different views in response to this statement.

Topic 4: Places and forms of worship

The Big Picture

In this Topic you will be examining Catholic places of worship; you will also be looking at some forms of worship. So you will study:

- cathedrals, churches and shrines
- the ways in which Catholics practise their faith in public
- personal and private rituals and customs practised at home or in private.

What?

You will:

- develop your knowledge and understanding of Catholic places of worship
- explain how Catholics use these places to worship God
- explain how Catholics worship God in private
- make links between these practices and how Catholics celebrate, reflect or worship.

Why?

Because:

- the architecture, decoration and care for places of worship help to make clear important Catholic beliefs
- understanding Catholic places and forms of worship can help you understand why Catholics think and act in the way they do
- understanding these places and practices helps you to compare and contrast how others, including yourself, worship.

How?

By:

- recalling and selecting information about Catholic places and forms of worship
- explaining their importance to Catholics today
- thinking about the relevance of Catholic buildings and forms of worship in 21st-century Britain
- evaluating your own views about these Catholic places and forms of worship.

Mass at St Peter's Basilica in the Vatican City, Italy.

GET STARTED

Think of the best thing that has ever happened to you. Now imagine that you have been given a large sum of money to build a lasting memorial to this thing. What would it be like? Where would it be? What would be in it? How would you decorate it? How would you care for it?

Develop your knowledge

Places and forms of worship

Catholic priests celebrate Mass every day.

KEY INFORMATION

- Catholics worship in many different places. Traditionally they worship in church buildings that are built in particular ways to reflect the important beliefs of those who worship there. These buildings are the focus of normal Sunday worship, but are also the place where other religious ceremonies and activities occur.
- Catholics use these buildings to mark important moments in their lives, like the birth of children (christenings), the joining of two people in marriage (weddings) and the celebration of a person's life on earth as they pass on into the next life (funerals). This means that churches have great significance for Catholic people.
- As these buildings are very special, great effort is made to decorate them with paintings and sculptures that depict important religious events or people. Churches are usually adorned with flowers to add colour and beauty. In solemn times, like Lent, flowers are kept to a minimum to remind the people of the suffering that is common in many lives.
- Worship occurs for Catholics in a variety of ways. The most common form of Catholic worship is the Mass which they are expected to attend once a week on Sundays and then on special occasions throughout the year, like Easter Sunday, Christmas Day, the Feast of All Saints and so on. (These days used to be called Holy Days of Obligation when Catholics were obliged to go to Mass.)
- Catholics are also expected to pray daily and may do this with others through smaller, more intimate ceremonies like Benediction. Many pray in private, kneeling down in a church, in a place of beauty or simply by sitting quietly in a special place. St Thérèse of Lisieux was known to pray whilst doing the washing-up, believing that everything a person does is a celebration of their life with God.

KEY QUESTIONS

KNOWLEDGE AND UNDERSTANDING

In what ways do Catholics worship?

What is meant by sacramental worship?

Why is the Mass so important to Catholics?

How do the architecture, layout and design of Catholic Churches help people to understand their beliefs?

What can be learned from Catholic places and forms of worship about special buildings, ceremonies or occasions?

ANALYSIS AND EVALUATION

'Catholics should go to church every Sunday to worship.' What do you think about this statement? How do you think Christians would respond to it?

KEY WORDS

absolution The pronouncement by a priest of the forgiveness of sins.

ceremony A formal procedure or service; specifically a religious ritual or service.

confession Contrition; penance. (i) One of seven sacraments observed by Catholics when a priest confidentially hears a person's confession. (ii) An admission, by a Christian, of wrong-doing. (iii) A particular official statement (or profession) of faith.

consecration The act of blessing the bread and wine, at which point God becomes present.

devotion Worship of a person, event or place that has special significance.

Eucharist Thanksgiving service celebrating the sacrificial death and resurrection of Jesus Christ; also known as Holy Communion or Mass.

host The special wafer-thin bread which represents Jesus' body in Holy Communion.

hymns Religious songs used during services, the words often being taken from the Bible.

lectern The stand in a church from which sacred texts are read.

Mary The Virgin Mary, Mother of Christ, Mother of God.

Mass A name for the Eucharist.

penance Part of the Sacrament of Reconciliation (see confesion).

prayer Speaking to God.

rosary String of prayer beads.

sacrament Religious rite or ceremony with special sacred significance.

sacred Holy; something or somewhere with particular religious meaning.

sermon Religious talk given by a priest or minister during services.

sin Act of rebellion or disobedience against the known will of God.

worship Pay respect or homage to someone or something.

FOR INTEREST

The origins of Catholic worship are found in the New Testament in the words and actions of Jesus. In the following quotation from the Gospel of St Mark, it is possible to see the beginnings of the practice of the Mass.

> *"Then, taking a cup, he gave thanks and said, 'Take this and share it among you, because from now on, I tell you, I shall never again drink wine until the kingdom of God comes.' Then he took bread, and when he had given thanks, he broke it and gave it to them, saying, 'This is my body given for you; do this in remembrance of me.' He did the same with the cup after supper, and said, 'This cup is the new covenant in my blood poured out for you.'"*
>
> (Luke 22:17–20)

Inside a Roman Catholic church

The next two pages will help you to:

- identify some of the most common features of the inside of a Catholic church
- make links between features of a church and key beliefs held by Roman Catholic Christians.

The Metropolitan Cathedral of Christ the King, Liverpool.

What would you expect to see in a Roman Catholic church?

In the past, most churches were built in the shape of a cross – this is called 'cruciform'. It reminds Christians that Jesus was put to death on a cross. The long part of the cross is usually aligned east–west, in the direction of Jerusalem. The main door is usually at the west end, or it may be in one of the shorter arms. The altar is usually at the eastern end, so the congregation will be facing the east. The eastern wall may also feature a large stained-glass window. This window will be brightly illuminated by the sun rising in the east.

AO1 skills ACTIVITIES

In pairs discuss all the features you would expect to see in a Catholic church. List these features in order of importance and explain why. Be prepared to explain your choices to the rest of the class.

At the entrance to the church, visitors will often find a baptismal font, used in the **Sacrament** of Baptism. The long arms of the cross form the nave of the church, and the short arms are called the transept. The point at which the nave and the transept cross is often topped with a spire, a tower or a dome.

Older church buildings have an altar against the eastern wall in a special part of the church called the sanctuary. When the priest was saying Mass at the altar, he had his back to the people as if he was leading them east towards Jerusalem (and by association, towards Jesus).

In the 1960s, it was agreed by the Second Vatican Council that it would be better if the priest faced the people and so altars were brought forward to the front of the sanctuary. During Mass the priest now carries out his **sacred** tasks with everyone able to see. Catholics believe that Jesus becomes present at the moment of the **consecration** (see Topic 4.4), so he is right in the centre of his people in the form of bread and wine.

Some churches take this symbolism further by building their place of **worship** in the round. A round church with its altar in the middle, like the Catholic Metropolitan Cathedral in Liverpool, gives a strong sense of Jesus at the heart of his community.

Some other features of a Catholic church include:

- the tabernacle – the special place where consecrated **hosts** are 'reserved' to be used in Masses or given as Holy Communion to the sick or housebound
- statues – religious sculptures of Mary, saints or special people associated with the particular church
- the sanctuary lamp – a special light that burns in front of the tabernacle when the Blessed Sacrament (consecrated bread) is inside
- a crucifix – a sculpted representation of Jesus on the cross as a reminder to Catholics that he died to save them all
- the lectern – a special stand from which readings from the Bible are given and from which the priest may deliver his sermons or the parish notices; sometimes the priest may give sermons from a raised platform or pulpit
- confessional – a small booth or stall used for the Sacrament of Reconciliation.

As well as being used for services, churches are often left open so that people can walk in at any time for a moment of peace and prayer or reflection. They might also want to light a candle to ask for help for someone who is ill or to remember someone who has died. Church buildings are also used by many members of the community for meetings and study or for prayer groups and social gatherings.

Cathedrals

Cathedrals are special church buildings. The name 'cathedral' comes from the latin word 'cathedra' which means seat or chair. A cathedral is where a Bishop has his chair. One obvious difference is that they tend to be much larger than churches. They can be very impressive buildings. Because of the Reformation (see Topics 3.4 and 3.5) most Catholic cathedrals in England are modern buildings. Each bishop of the Church will have a cathedral as the central church of their region, or diocese.

RESEARCH NOTE

Using an encyclopaedia, dictionary or the Internet, look up 'altar'. What is the purpose of an altar? What ceremonies are carried out on altars? Why might Catholics need an altar in their church?

AO2 skills ACTIVITIES

Christians worship in special buildings. How might a Catholic defend having a special place to worship when they believe that God is everywhere? What advantages do you think are gained by worshipping in a specially designed building? Write a script of an interview between two people who differ in their views and role-play it back to the class.

You have been asked to design a new church. As the architect, what features would you make a priority and what materials would you use? Make a sketch of your building or draw a plan of the layout. Be prepared to explain to the class how your design would aid worship.

Religious art

The next two pages will help you to:

- recognise different forms of Catholic religious art
- understand the contribution of art in communicating important Catholic beliefs
- evaluate the role of Catholic religious art.

Art in places of worship

Religious art is often appreciated by people with no relationship with Christianity – you only need to see the thousands of people flocking to the Sistine Chapel in Rome to understand this. They go with the intention of seeing Michelangelo's amazing paintings on the ceiling. The original reasons why these great works of art were created were either to help people to **worship** God, to present complicated beliefs to ordinary people, or simply to praise God for the wonders of the creation.

Religious paintings or images

In most Catholic churches there will be a number of religious paintings or images. Some show images of Jesus from his life on earth. Others depict Mary or one of the other saints. Some will show events in the lives of other holy women and men. Some common types of painting include the Madonna (Mary holding the baby Jesus), the Pietà (Mary cradling Jesus' dead body after it was taken down from the cross) and Calvary (an image of Jesus on the cross, surrounded by the two others being executed and soldiers).

There may also be stained-glass windows which tell stories from the Bible and of the saints. In the past, when most people could not read, these were a way in which they learnt and remembered religious stories.

Icons

More commonly associated with Eastern traditions of Christianity such as the Russian Orthodox, icons are paintings on wooden blocks and depict scenes from the life of Jesus and the saints. Traditionally icons can be of the transfiguration – the sudden appearance of radiant light emanating from Jesus Christ while he stood with Moses and Elijah, recorded in the Bible as happening on a mountaintop in front of three of his disciples – the nativity or the resurrection. Some of this art is very beautiful and has been adopted by some Catholics as a focus for their worship. The icon becomes a 'doorway to the **sacred**'.

Statues

Statues also provide a 'doorway to the sacred' as they can be the focus of **devotion** for those who find help for their faith in the stories of particular holy men and women. Often a church will have a statue of its patron saint somewhere inside. For example, a church dedicated to St Martin de Porres might have a statue of Martin, one of the world's first black saints. Similarly, a church named St Theresa's might be named after Teresa of Ávila or Thérèse of Lisieux.

AO1 skills ACTIVITIES

Remember a significant event in your life. What happened? How did you feel? Jesus' last journey to the cross was full of powerful moments. Consider the Stations of the Cross. Which three stations help you best to understand how Jesus was feeling? Be prepared to explain your choices.

RESEARCH NOTE

Find out about the life and works of Michelangelo. How many paintings did he create? For whom did he create them? Did he make as much money as an artist would today?

A stained-glass window showing Jesus as the 'Lamb of God' (John 1:29).

St Peter's Basilica in Rome has a vast statue of St Peter possibly made by Arnolfo di Cambio in about 1300 CE. The feet of the statue have been worn smooth by the hands of the millions of people who have touched it in honour over the many years it has stood there.

Statues often feature in shrines, which are special places where particular holy men and women are commemorated.

Stations of the Cross

Around the walls of a Catholic church there is usually a series of special paintings or carvings which depict scenes from the passion of Jesus (the events in the last hours of his life leading up to his crucifixion). During Lent, these images become the focus for worship. There are usually fourteen images in the Stations of the Cross:

1. Jesus in the Garden of Gethsemane
2. Jesus is betrayed by Judas and arrested
3. Jesus is condemned by the Sanhedrin
4. Jesus is denied by Peter
5. Jesus is judged by Pilate
6. Jesus is scourged and crowned with thorns
7. Jesus takes up his cross
8. Jesus is helped by Simon to carry his cross
9. Jesus meets the women of Jerusalem
10. Jesus is crucified
11. Jesus promises his kingdom to the good thief
12. Jesus entrusts Mary and John to each other
13. Jesus dies on the cross
14. Jesus is laid in the tomb

Some churches have a 15th station which marks the resurrection. There are different sets of Stations of the Cross. This set was approved by Pope Benedict XVI in 2007.

One of the Stations of the Cross in Westminster Cathedral, London, carved by the sculptor Eric Gill in 1918.

MUST THINK ABOUT!

Think about Pontius Pilate condemning Jesus to death. What made him do this? Discuss this with a friend. Does this image capture the horror of what was about to happen to Jesus?

AO2 skills ACTIVITIES

Create a leaflet for primary school children identifying and explaining the importance of the art they might see in a Catholic church. If you have access to a computer you could add images to your leaflet or draw them yourself.

Some Christians think statues and paintings are a distraction and hinder people from the worship of God. What do you think a Catholic would say in response? Role-play or script an interview where two Christians explore their different points of view.

Public acts of worship 1: Mass

The next two pages will help you to:

- examine the important aspects of Catholic Mass
- identify the rituals of the Mass
- identify the important biblical events that are recalled in the Mass.

The Mass has two parts: the Liturgy of the Word which has Bible readings and the Liturgy of the Eucharist.

The Eucharist

Read the **sacred** text in the box, which describes what happened at Emmaus, shortly after Jesus' resurrection.

Luke 24:30–32

Now while he was with them at table, he took the bread and said the blessing; then he broke it and handed it to them. And their eyes were opened and they recognised him; but he had vanished from their sight. Then they said to each other, 'Did not our hearts burn within us as he talked to us on the road and explained the scriptures to us?'

Eucharist comes from a Greek word meaning 'thanksgiving'. At the end of the story of Emmaus the two men are said to have 'recognised him (Jesus)' at the breaking of bread. This action is repeated at Mass to remind Catholics of what Jesus also did at the Last Supper (see Topic 2.2). Jesus' breaking of bread was a symbolic action which represented the breaking of his body on the cross. The pouring of wine at the Last Supper represented the blood he was to shed.

AO1 skills ACTIVITIES

Make an acrostic from the word 'Eucharist' by writing the letters vertically in the centre of your book. Form sentences around each letter that explain different parts of the Mass.

REMEMBER THIS

After the priest has received the offertory, he washes his hands with the help of the altar servers. As well as symbolising the need to purify himself before performing the consecration, it is an ancient custom possibly arising from when he would have been made dirty by all the things the congregation had brought in as their offering for the week.

Each action of the Mass, therefore, recalls something powerful in Jesus' passion. It seems strange to give praise and thanks for something that was so sad and painful but, for Catholics (and other Christians), Jesus' suffering and death made it possible for the resurrection to occur. The Mass commemorates Jesus' four actions: taking, blessing, breaking and sharing.

Taking

At a Catholic Mass, there is always an offertory, which is the time when people give gifts to the Church. As well as money that is collected, they also present the priest with gifts of bread and wine. In the past, people would have given other produce such as food, cattle, vegetables – whatever they could give from their work. The priest 'takes' these gifts to offer them up to God.

Blessing

Through their ordination, priests are given special powers that allow them to bless the bread and wine in an act of **consecration**, while reciting one part of the Eucharistic prayer. Catholics believe that at this point, God becomes present in the church. This is a very holy moment and the congregation may kneel as a sign of respect.

Breaking

It is important to remember that for Catholics, Jesus and God are one and the same. For them, God is made present by the sanctification (making holy) of the gifts by the priest but also by his repetition of the actions of Jesus at the Last Supper and Emmaus, when he took bread, blessed it and broke it.

Sharing

At the Last Supper and at Emmaus Jesus is reported to have shared food with his apostles and disciples. It is only fitting therefore that the bread and wine given in his memory should be shared with the people now that they have become his body and blood. This is a very special moment in the Mass and should be treated with the utmost respect. Holy Communion brings the whole Catholic family together, united in the action of Jesus.

REMEMBER THIS

The four actions have technical names which you could use to impress examiners. Taking is known as oblation; blessing as consecration; breaking as fraction; sharing as communion. Using these words could get you a higher grade. If you can explain 'transubstantiation', another technical word, you could get more credit. It is made up of two Latin words which mean 'across' and 'substance'. The word is used to describe the mystery by which bread and wine have their substance changed to flesh and blood, though they appear unchanged.

AO2 skills ACTIVITIES

The gifts of bread and wine are central to the celebration of the Mass. Explain their importance and consider whether or not their meaning is still relevant and understood today.

Examine the reasons why some Christians celebrate the Mass more frequently than others. In what ways do you think attending weekly Mass might strengthen people's faith?

Public acts of worship 2: Mass

The next two pages will help you to:

- explain the origins of rituals within the Mass
- identify some of the important artefacts and objects that are used in the Mass and explain their religious significance.

The articles used for celebrating Mass.

AO1 skills ACTIVITIES

Identify the different parts of the Mass and draw up a table of what happens and where. If you have access to a computer you could insert or draw symbols, vestments and sacred vessels to decorate your table.

Celebrating Mass

Mass is celebrated in a variety of ways. Until the 1960s, Mass was always said in Latin so that wherever a Catholic went in the world they would be able to understand what was happening. Since the late 1960s, Mass has usually been said in the vernacular (the language of the people attending it), so English is used in Great Britain or the USA, Polish in Poland, Portuguese in Brazil and so on. Some people prefer a quiet, peaceful Mass early in the morning whereas others prefer hymns or songs of celebration to aid their **worship**.

MUST THINK ABOUT!

The readings are read at the lectern. There is usually one reading from the Old Testament, a Psalm, a reading from the New Testament and a reading from one of the gospels. Often the gospel reading is performed by a priest or deacon, while the other readings may be read by a lay person (someone who is not an ordained member of the clergy). Do you think a lay person should be given special training before they read at Mass?

In addition to the four actions of the Mass you studied in Topic 4.3, there are always readings from the Bible, whatever the style of the worship. At Sunday Mass, and on other high days and holy days, the priest will preach a sermon which explains the readings or comments on other aspects of Catholic life. In a parish Mass, there will often be local notices given out or the celebration of other aspects of family life, like christenings.

At some point in the Mass there will always be a time for private prayer and for formal prayers that the whole congregation recites. Bidding prayers are written by the people (sometimes referred to as the prayers of the faithful) and are usually prayers asking for God for help (petition) with events in the world, sickness, death or suffering of some sort. After Communion, thanksgiving prayers are said in private and as a community.

The artefacts of Mass

There are a number of special artefacts or objects used at a Mass:

- candles – to symbolise Jesus as the light of the world and to show God's presence in the Mass
- chalice – the special cup which contains the wine
- ciborium – the special vessel which holds the **host** (special wafer thin bread)
- cruets – the vessels which contain wine and water to be used in the **Eucharist**
- special torches – carried by altar servers to symbolise the presence of God
- thurible – a vessel for burning incense which, at a 'high' Mass, is used to symbolise the offerings rising in a cloud towards God.

The people involved in the Mass

There are a number of people who carry out special roles during a Mass:

- altar servers – the people who help the priest with the Mass and contribute to the ceremonial aspects of it, such as processions
- cantor – someone who leads the congregation in song
- choir – people who provide singing to lead the congregation
- flower arrangers – whose work is done before Mass but who make an important contribution to the dignity and solemnity of the occasion
- musicians – not every church has an organist; some congregations prefer different styles of music to lead their singing
- organist – the person who plays an organ to accompany the congregation's singing
- readers – the people who read from the Bible
- sidesmen – those people who take up the collection or count the people present when a census is being taken.

Each of these people is said to have a ministry. For the rest of the congregation, ministry may be something that they do away from the church, maybe just by representing God in their daily lives and work.

RESEARCH NOTE

Visit a local Catholic church and ask if you can see and take photos of the objects and artefacts that are used at Mass. Use the photos to create a presentation of all the things you have seen and photographed.

AO2 skills ACTIVITIES

A friend gives you five reasons why attending Mass on Sundays is a waste of time. What might these reasons be and what arguments would you use in defence of attending weekly Mass?

Every celebration of the Mass ends with the instruction to go out into the world to love and serve the Lord. Compare and contrast the different ways Catholics might try to follow this instruction.

Public acts of worship 3

The next two pages will help you to:

- explore other forms of worship in Catholicism
- develop your understanding of the origins of these forms of worship
- evaluate these forms of worship from your own point of view.

Benediction

In Topics 4.3 and 4.4 you read about the Mass and how Jesus comes to be present in the form of bread and wine. You also read that the tabernacle is the place in the church where consecrated hosts are stored, since they contain the real presence of Jesus.

There is a special and ancient **ceremony** called Benediction in which Jesus is shown to the faithful. A large consecrated host is placed inside a glass box called a lunette and then into a monstrance, which is an object usually in the shape of a sunburst. Monstrances are usually very ornate and are treated with the utmost care since Catholics believe they are carrying Jesus. The name of this object has its origins in the Latin word meaning 'to show'. The priest covers his hands with a special ceremonial cloak called a humeral veil, before touching the monstrance.

As the priest lifts the monstrance, the congregation kneel as a mark of respect for Jesus as they believe he has come among them. At the same time, one of the altar servers will cense the monstrance, to symbolise the prayers of the faithful rising up to God as well as recreating the clouds of glory that used to accompany Jesus in his earthly life.

AO1 skills ACTIVITIES

Spend in few minutes in silence passing a circle of string through your fingers. How does this make you feel? Do you feel calmer and that you are concentrating more after doing it? Why do you think you feel as you do?

Rosary

The Rosary is one of the most common forms of informal prayer. It is also used extensively as a collective act of **worship**. Possibly invented by St Dominic in the 12th century as a means of meditating on episodes in the life of Jesus, seen through the eyes of his mother, **Mary**, the Rosary is a series of prayers recited in an almost chant-like style.

People 'praying the Rosary' use a set of beads to keep count of the prayers that they are saying. Each set of beads has five sets of ten beads to represent the Hail Marys to be said – this is called a decade. These are separated by a single bead which reminds the person to say an Our Father and a Glory Be between the decades. At the end of the loop is a short length of beads which lead down to a crucifix. Further prayers are said, finishing with the Apostles' Creed as a statement of the faith of the person praying.

Each decade of the rosary represents an event in the life of Jesus, called 'mysteries'. There are now twenty mysteries that are recalled, falling into one of four categories, as shown in the table.

AO2 skills ACTIVITIES

Evaluate the importance of saying grace after meals. Do you think it is important or not? Give reasons for your answer and explain how a Catholic might respond to the question.

Joyful	Luminous	Sorrowful	Glorious
The Annunciation	The Baptism in the Jordan	The Agony in the Garden	The Resurrection
The Visitation to Elizabeth	The Wedding at Cana	The Scourging at the Pillar	The Ascension
The Nativity (birth of Jesus)	The Proclamation of the Kingdom	Jesus is crowned with thorns	The Coming of the Holy Spirit
The Presentation in the Temple	The Transfiguration	The carrying of the Cross	The Assumption of Mary into Heaven
The Finding in the Temple	The Institution of the Eucharist	The crucifixion	The Crowning of Mary, Queen of Heaven

Angelus

A common feature of Catholic churches is the bell tower. Many European countries continue the ancient custom of ringing the bell at noon. The bell is a reminder that Catholics should stop what they are doing and recite a prayer called the Angelus. The name comes from the first word of the prayer which starts, 'The angel of the Lord appeared unto Mary...' Those who cannot remember the words are encouraged to say the Hail Mary five times instead. The Angelus is often said in the morning and in the evening by devout Catholics.

There are even schools which stop at noon so that everyone can say the Angelus together. Many schools which do this also stop before lunchtime to say 'grace'. Grace comes from the Latin word which means 'thanks', and so those who say grace before meals are thanking God for the gift of food. Saying grace is not confined to Catholics, and members of many other denominations will use it as a common form of worship in their homes.

The bell tower of the cathedral of Santa Maria del Fiore (The Duomo) in Florence, Italy.

Private acts of worship

The next two pages will help you to:

- explain what prayer is
- give examples of the reasons why Christians pray.

Prayer is an opportunity to spend time with God.

AO1 skills ACTIVITIES

The Lord's Prayer is one that almost all Christians use regularly and will know off by heart. It contains some key beliefs about God. Read the prayer through again and discuss with a partner what you think each line is saying about what Christians believe. Now write your own version in a more modern style. You could even try this in 'txt' language. Share what you have done with the rest of the class to see the range of styles and interpretations that the class has come up with.

What is prayer?

Prayer is a way in which Christians try to communicate with God. The ways in which Christians do this are many and varied. It may be an internal conversation that a Christian will have with God, or it may take the the form of a traditional prayer; it may be spoken or silent. All forms of prayer are ways in which Christians aim to develop their own personal relationship with God.

Jesus did not give his Disciples many instructions regarding how they should pray. He himself attended the synagogue to **worship** alongside other Jews. When asked how people should pray Jesus responded that they should pray behind closed doors and, when alone, in secret. Many Christians spend time praying in this way. Jesus also gave his followers 'The Lord's Prayer'.

The Lord's Prayer (Missal)

Our Father, who art in heaven,
hallowed be thy name;
Thy kingdom come;
Thy will be done on earth as it is in heaven. Give us this day our daily bread;
and forgive us our trespasses as we forgive those who trespass against us;
and lead us not into temptation,
but deliver us from evil.

Most Catholics will pray in **church** alongside their fellow believers. Prayer is a central part of church services and many would include 'The Lord's Prayer'. Over the years other prayers have been written down which express Christian beliefs. Catholics used a book called a Missal, which contains these. Reading the Bible is also a form of prayer.

Matthew 6:5–6

And when you pray, do not imitate the hypocrites: they love to say their prayers standing up in the synagogues and at the street corners for people to see them. In truth I tell you, they have had their reward. But when you pray, go into your room, shut yourself in, and so pray to your Father who is in that secret place, and your Father who sees all that is done in secret will reward you.

The Gloria

The Gloria is a formal prayer that is used frequently by Catholics in **worship** and in their private prayer life. 'Glory be to the Father, the Son and Holy Spirit, as it was in the beginning, is now and ever shall be, world without end. Amen.'

This prayer contains within it some important statements of belief. It reminds Catholics of the Trinity, of the creation and of a future life in Heaven. These are three core beliefs and are some of the reasons why Catholics wish to give glory to God.

The Divine Office

All priests are required to pray formally every day using what is called the Divine Office. Some lay people choose to make this prayer voluntarily. As well as reciting the familiar prayers mentioned above, this form of worship includes readings from the Psalms and other parts of the **sacred** scriptures. In monastic communities the Divine Office takes place as part of a daily cycle of prayers that even interrupts their sleep.

Types of prayer

There are many reasons why people pray. These could depend on what is happening in a person's life at that time and sometimes people pray for many reasons all at once. At other times they will have a special focus. Some of the most common reasons are:

- **To thank God**: Christians believe that God is responsible for the world around them, He is all-powerful and all-knowing, the Creator. Because they believe this Christians will often thank God for the world around them and everything they believe that he has done for them. This type of prayer is also called Thanksgiving.
- **To praise God**: This type of prayer recognises that God is beyond human understanding and it worthy of worship. It reminds Christians of God's greatness. This type of prayer is also called Adoration.
- **To say sorry to God**: When a person feels that they have done something that has gone against what they believe and that they have in some way let themselves and God down, they may pray to say sorry. This type of prayer is called Confession.
- **To ask for God's help**: When people feel the need for help, perhaps when things have gone wrong for them and they feel that God may be able to help them, giving them strength, they will pray in this way. They may also ask for his intervention in the world, for example to help someone who is ill. This type of prayer is called Supplication.

AO1 skills ACTIVITIES

Prayers are like poems. They help believers to express what it is important to them. Think about what is important to you. This might be your friends, your family, a hobby or a religious belief. Now compose a poem or prayer about what you find important in your life. You might want to keep this private and personal.

Sacraments

The next two pages will help you to:

- identify the seven sacraments of the Catholic Church
- identify the most important aspects of the Sacrament of Reconciliation
- explain why 'going to confession' is an important part of the spiritual life of Catholics
- evaluate the reasons for or against the Catholic practice of 'going to confession'.

The seven sacraments of the Catholic Church

Saint Augustine (354–430 CE) said that a sacrament was 'the outward visible form of an inner invisible grace'. The most important sacrament is the Eucharist because Catholics believe that it is a channel of grace to believers who receive the body and blood of Jesus in the bread and wine.

The Catholic Church has seven sacraments:

- Eucharist (see Topics 4.3 and 4.4)
- Baptism (see Topic 5.6)
- Confirmation (see Topic 3.6)
- Marriage (see Topic 5.7)
- Reconciliation (see below)
- Ordination (see Topic 5.8)
- Anointing the Sick (see Topic 5.9).

The Sacrament of Reconciliation

The **Sacrament** of Reconciliation is a **ceremony** which is sometimes called **Confession**, **Absolution** and **Penance**. Officially it is called the Sacrament of Reconciliation because it enables a Catholic to be reconciled with God. What does it mean to be 'reconciled with God'?

Many Catholics go to confession every week.

The fall from grace and sin

Genesis 3:6

The woman saw that the tree was good to eat and pleasing to the eye, and that it was enticing for the wisdom that it could give. So she took some of its fruit and ate it. She also gave some to her husband who was with her, and he ate it.

In the story of the Garden of Eden, Adam is said to have 'fallen from grace'. He was tempted by Eve and **sinned** by eating the fruit of the tree of the knowledge of good and evil. The story is symbolic: the word 'Adam' is the Hebrew word for 'human beings'. This means that, if the Bible is taken to be literally true, all humanity walked in the garden and thus all humanity sinned.

Catholics do not regard the Bible as literally true; rather it is a collection of symbolic stories of which the story of the Garden of Eden is one. Catholics do believe, however, that sin is a fact of life and part of the human condition. Although human beings are made in the image and likeness of God (the perfect being), sometimes their behaviour is not perfect but is sinful.

AO1 skills ACTIVITIES

Make a list of the things that you would like to be forgiven for. These might be things that you did but should not have done or things that you did not do but should have. Look again at the list and consider what you ought to do in order to apologise for these things.

Sin is about breaking a relationship with someone or something. Catholics believe therefore that a sin against someone is a sin against God, and just as the human relationship needs to be restored, so the sinner's relationship with God needs to be reconciled.

The four stages of reconciliation

Reconciliation has four stages:

- examination of conscience
- confession
- absolution
- penance.

Examination of conscience

Before you can say sorry it is essential to recognise what you have done wrong, so Catholics will spend some time in private prayer reflecting on this before going to confession. Some use a set meditation to help organise their thoughts.

Confession

Either in private, in a confessional (a special room set aside for the celebration of this sacrament) or face to face with a priest, the person recalls their sins and explains why they are sorry for what they have done. The technical word for their sorrow is 'contrition'. Often the priest will give advice or talk through with the person what they could do to avoid committing the sin again.

Absolution

When the priest has heard the person's confession and can tell that they are genuinely sorry, they absolve them. This is a spiritual way of 'wiping the slate clean' and only priests have the power to do it. They get this power when they are ordained by the bishop. In religious terms, they have the power to release people from their sins.

Penance

The sacrament is complete when the person undertakes a punishment given to them by the priest. The technical word for this is 'penance' and a person who is going through penance is called a 'penitent'. In the past penances varied from having to give up sexual relations for a year to making a pilgrimage across dangerous territory. Today penances tend to be more positive and might involve additional daily prayers or carrying out charitable deeds. In some ways, it is about restoring the relationship broken by the sinful act, by balancing up the scales between good and evil.

MUST THINK ABOUT!

Listen to the words of 'Sorry' by Tracy Chapman or Westlife, or 'Sorry Seems to be the Hardest Word' by Elton John or Blue. Do you understand what these songwriters are trying to say?

AO2 skills ACTIVITIES

'People should tell God that they are sorry; they don't need to go to a priest, who is just another human being.' Do you agree with this? How might a Catholic respond?

The importance and effect of worship

The next two pages will help you to:

- show your knowledge of the effect of worship on Catholics
- explain the effect of some rituals on Catholics
- evaluate the influence of participation in worship on their personal life.

CAFOD
just one world

ONE RACE • THE HUMAN RACE
carj
Catholic Association for Racial Justice

PROGRESSIO
CHANGING MINDS • CHANGING LIVES

A state of grace

'Go in peace to love and serve the Lord.' These are the words with which the priest closes Mass. They imply that a person who has been to Mass and participated in Holy Communion is in a better state than when they arrived. In the past this was called a 'state of grace'. Catholics are said to be in a state of grace when they have taken one of the **sacraments**, the most obvious being the Sacrament of Reconciliation, since this takes away their **sin**.

AO1 skills ACTIVITIES

Discuss with a partner. Do you have a special day of the week that is different from the other days? Explain why this day is special to you. Compare your responses with other people.

Living with the moral teachings

Like many other Christians, Catholics who attend church on Sunday should behave in accordance with the moral teachings of the Church at all times, otherwise they risk being accused of hypocrisy. This means that they should:

- do to other people only what they would have others do to them (Jesus' golden rule)
- care for, respect and treat others as if they were sisters or brothers
- care for the creation and everything in it
- only take part in work or activities that bear witness to the Kingdom of God
- bear witness to the Kingdom of God through their attitude and behaviour.

Many Catholics choose to work in occupations that enable them to bear witness, perhaps teaching, nursing or one of the other caring professions. Others bring their Catholic principles or beliefs to bear in their daily work. Some work directly for organisations committed to justice like the Catholic Institute for International Relations (CIIR), Live Simply, the Catholic Association for Racial Justice (CARJ), the Catholic Fund for Overseas Development (CAFOD) or the LIFE movement. By doing this, many are making real the Catholic axiom 'to work is to pray'.

Effect of worship on daily lives

In other smaller ways Christians show the effect of worship on their daily lives. On Sundays, some will choose to participate only in activities that are based around going to church or being with the family. Others will set aside time during the day to pray or to go to a church. Most Christians give money to the Church through the Sunday collection, some even give a tenth of their income. This derives from the ancient custom of 'tithing', when the ordinary people gave a tenth of their wages to the Church.

Many Catholics will have times for prayer at home when the family come together to worship.

It is a central Catholic belief that it is not possible to separate daily life from its sources of spiritual support. Catholics are therefore expected to behave the same on Mondays as they do on Sundays.

FOR DEBATE

Have a whole-class discussion around the following statement: 'It doesn't matter what a Christian does at work, as long as they go to church on Sunday.' (If you want to, replace 'work' with 'school'.) Where are the boundaries between daily and spiritual life? Can a Catholic ignore his or her beliefs when they go out into the world?

AO2 skills ACTIVITIES

'People should only worship God when they want to, not because they have been told to.' Do you agree with this statement? How would a Catholic respond to this?

GradeStudio

Welcome to the Grade Studio

GCSE is about what you can do, not what you can't do. You need to know what examiners want in your answers so that you can get the best possible marks. In GCSE Religious Studies there are two things that examiners are looking for. These are called assessment objectives (AO). Questions are designed to help examiners find out how well you do in each assessment objective.

Graded examples for this topic

AO1

AO1 questions test what you know and how well you can explain and analyse things. Let's look at an AO1 question to see what examiners are expecting you to do.

Question

Describe two features of a place of worship and explain their importance. **[6 marks]**

Possible steps to answer the question: What should an answer be like and how do examiners work out what is a good or a poor response?

This is an AO1 question, meaning it is trying to test your knowledge and understanding. Examiners will use three levels to measure how successfully you demonstrate these skills.

First of all, choose two features which have clear religious importance. This might be practical or spiritual importance, or even location in the building. You may not be able to say as much about one feature as the other, but this does not matter as response will be marked by levels; examiners will judge the whole response and not break it into two responses of three marks each.

Student's answer	Examiner's comment
Two features in most churches are a font to baptise babies in and an altar to celebrate Mass on.	The candidate has identified two features but the details and explanations are lacking clarity and accuracy (Level 1).

Student's answer	Examiner's comment
Christian churches usually have a font and an altar. The font is often near the door as a sign of welcoming the baby into the faith, and the altar, the special table where the bread and wine is changed into the body and blood of Christ, is in the centre of the sanctuary for all to see.	The candidate has written a satisfactory answer. They name and explain two common items and show a depth of religious understanding concerning their function (Level 2).

Student's improved answer	Examiner's comment
Christian churches usually have a font and an altar. The font is often near the door as a sign of welcoming the baby into the faith. It holds the water which is used to cleanse the baby from sin during the Sacrament of Baptism. The altar reminds Christians of the table used at the Last Supper by Jesus. This was the first time the bread and the wine were changed into the body and blood of Jesus. Catholics celebrate the Eucharist or thanksgiving at every Mass.	The candidate has written a good answer. They name and explain two common items and explain in detail their purpose and symbolism using correct religious language such as sacrament and Eucharist (Level 3).

AO2

Question

Evaluate the statement: 'Christians should not need a special building for worship.' **[12 marks]**

Before responding to the statement, identify the key words in it. Here the key words are 'should' and 'need'. You could use a spider diagram to note down all the possible views that you might wish to use. Examiners use four levels for AO2, which means they can evaluate muddled responses, but it is better to be well organised as that will ensure you reach the highest levels more easily.

Student's answer

Christians believe that God is everywhere, so they don't need to go to church. They can pray in their own bedrooms or on their way to places such as work or school. Large churches cost a lot of money and this could be given to the poor.

Examiner's comment

The candidate has written one statement and given several supporting reasons (Level 2).

Student's answer

Some Christians believe that because God is everywhere they do not need to go to church to worship him. Everyone is busy and church services are not always at the best times for families. Some Christians are too sick or old to attend. Other Christians believe that going to church supports their faith because they are with like-minded people. At church they hear the Word of God and receive Holy Communion. I believe the one hour a week is not that much to give up.

Examiner's comment

The candidate has written a good answer. They have included two different points of view and have given supporting arguments for both. They have used religious language correctly. They have also given a personal viewpoint (Level 3).

Student's improved answer

Christians believe that God is everywhere, but most think it is best to worship him in church with other Christians. They believe this because Jesus often went to the synagogue to hear the scriptures and to the temple at Passover. Christianity is about loving God and loving one's neighbour and you cannot do this alone. Catholics believe that they need to receive Holy Communion regularly and hear the Word of God. On the other hand, there are some Christians who believe they can worship God anywhere and read the Bible in their own homes. Maybe they do, but most people need to go to church to help them in their faith. Churches have statues and special features which aid worship. Many people like to sing hymns and listen to the sermon. I believe that one hour a week is not that much to give up, considering Jesus' sacrifice of his life for us.

Examiner's comment

The candidate has written several valid arguments for and against the statement. They have referred to the example set by Jesus and explained how Christianity is a communal, not individual, religion. They have supported their own point of view with an additional reason (Level 4).

These specimen answers provide an outline of how you could construct your response. Space does not allow us to give a full response. The examiner will be looking for more detail in your actual exam responses.

Remember and Reflect

AO1 Describe, explain and analyse, using knowledge and understanding

	Find the answer on:
1 Name five different places of worship used by Catholics.	PAGE 92
2 Explain the function of a cathedral.	PAGE 95
3 Give definitions of the following words: *a* *worship* *b* *ceremony* *c* *devotion*	PAGE 93
4 Explain what happens on an altar at Mass.	PAGE 98–99
5 What is the purpose of a lectern?	PAGE 95
6 Explain how some Catholics use statues as a focus for their worship.	PAGE 96
7 Describe how a Catholic may follow the Stations of the Cross.	PAGE 97
8 How are holy women and men sometimes depicted in religious art?	PAGE 96
9 Identify four actions that the priest carries out during the Eucharist.	PAGE 99
10 Identify the seven sacraments.	PAGE 106
11 What is the 'vernacular'?	PAGE 100
12 Make a list of some of the roles that can be fulfilled by lay people associated with the Mass.	PAGE 101
13 What is an act of contrition?	PAGE 107
14 Write the names of three formal prayers said regularly by Catholics in private or at Mass.	PAGE 104–105
15 What effect do Catholic beliefs have on the architecture of their places of worship? Give some examples of how this is reflected in practice.	PAGE 93–94

AO2 Use evidence and reasoned argument to express and evaluate personal responses, informed insights, and differing viewpoints

1 'Cathedrals are monuments to the people who paid for them to be built.'

'Cathedrals are a magnificent way of human beings paying respect to the glory of God.'

Evaluate each of these statements. Choose the one that is closest to your view and explain why.

2 Do you think it is easier to pray in a place where there are many signs and symbols to help you or is it better to pray somewhere where there are no distractions and you can talk directly to God? Provide reasons for your answer and relate it to your own experience, even if you do not regularly pray.

3 If you had something on your conscience, would you prefer to tell a doctor, a psychologist, a social worker, a friend, your parents or a priest? Give reasons for your answer, including reasons why you do not prefer the others.

4 Complete the table with your analysis of each of the forms of worship mentioned and say whether people would use it as a private or public religious activity.

Form of worship	Private	Public
Taking Communion		
Saying the Rosary		
Benediction		
Praying the Our Father		

5 Do you think it is important for Catholics to go to Mass every Sunday? What might be the benefits of doing this? What might be the disadvantages?

6 It is often said that belief in God has been the inspiration for some of the finest works of art: painting, sculpture, dance, drama and music. Do you agree or disagree? Explain your thinking.

7 What do you think of religious orders that separate themselves from the world in order to pray for its conversion? Do you think this is a good use of a vocation?

Topic 5: Religion in the faith community and the family

The Big Picture

In this Topic you will be examining how religion is celebrated in and around the community and how it is celebrated and shared in the family. You will be studying:

- the important rites and ceremonies that Catholics use to mark the stages of a person's life
- the meaning of 'community' and what it means to live in a community
- the distinctive features of a Catholic community.

What?

You will:

- explore how key moments in a Catholic's life are celebrated
- examine how Catholic communities are formed
- evaluate Catholic practices against your own life experiences.

Why?

Because:

- knowing about and understanding Catholic 'rites of passage' will help you to appreciate the choices Catholics make
- understanding how Catholic communities are formed and organised provides an insight into their morality
- evaluating Catholic practice can enable you to make informed judgements about your own lifestyle and personal choices.

How?

By:

- studying Catholic rituals, customs and practices
- discussing these religious acts in class and with your friends and family
- carrying out investigative work on each of these sub-topics.

After a requiem mass the coffin is taken to the cemetery for burial.

GET STARTED

'All Christians have a responsibility to help the poor.' Do you agree or disagree? Give reasons. Do a survey to find out whether people are really concerned about making sure the things they buy, food and clothes for example, have been fairly traded.

Develop your knowledge

Religion in the faith community and the family

Religious orders of both monks and nuns are an important part of Catholic life.

KEY INFORMATION

- The Catholic Church is a worldwide community. In every country across the globe there are Catholics who share the same beliefs, perform the same rites and behave in the same ways as Catholics in your town. The Greek word 'catholic' means universal. Catholicism is an organisation with members around the world. For Catholics, this means that on a Sunday, as long as they can find a church, they will be able to attend Mass and know what is happening.
- There are many types of community founded on Catholic principles and values. For example, monastic communities were often founded by a devout person who believed that grouping men or women together to pray, work and live together

KEY QUESTIONS

KNOWLEDGE AND UNDERSTANDING

To what extent does Catholicism present models for family living?

What are the main rites and practices within Catholicism that mark the passages from one stage of life to another?

ANALYSIS AND EVALUATION

What does it mean to live in a community?

What influence does knowledge and understanding of Catholic community living have on relationships and behaviour?

would be a good way of building the Kingdom of God on earth. Among the founders of the world's great religious communities were St Benedict (Benedictines), St Dominic (Dominicans), St Francis (Franciscans) and St Simon Stock (Carmelites).

- Today it is possible to live in a religious community without taking the vows of a person joining a religious order. Lay communities are made up of people who have not taken holy orders (been ordained) or taken sacred vows.
- The practice of living in a community has its origins in the early Christian Church that was made up of Jesus' apostles, some of the women who followed him and other disciples. There are many stories of this community in the Acts of the Apostles.

KEY WORDS

apostle One of the twelve of Jesus' closest disciples. 'Apostle' means 'one who is sent' and is the name given, therefore, to those who were sent out by Jesus to preach, to baptise and to gather the people into a Church.

baptism The sacrament that marks a person's joining the Church. This rite of initiation involves immersion in, or sprinkling or pouring of, water.

christening The practice of infant baptism, when a child is brought into the family of the Church by its parents.

confirmation The sacrament that marks the choice an adult makes to participate fully in the life of the Church.

disciple A follower. The disciples referred to in the gospels and in the Acts of the Apostles were followers of Jesus.

domestic church The family, the place where Catholics pray, work and live together.

laity Ordinary members of the Church (not a priest, monk, nun, religious sister or religious brother).

matrimony Marriage; one of the seven sacraments.

monastic A community of monks or nuns living together.

ordination The 'laying on of hands' on priests and deacons by a bishop, giving priests the power to offer absolution.

parish A local community of Christians grouped together in a geographical region.

religious order An organised group of monks or nuns, often founded by one of the great saints of the Church.

- 'Praying, living, and working together' is a good description of the ideal Catholic family. Catholics have a strong sense of family life and see the home as the most important community of the faithful – it is sometimes even referred to as the domestic Church.
- When a new member of the family is born there is often a celebration. For Catholics this is called baptism and marks their entry into the Church. It is also called a christening. Confirmation is the ceremony that older Catholics choose to go through as a public statement of their decision to participate as an adult member of the Church.
- The place where Christians meet regularly to worship is the church. Usually this building is at the geographical heart of a local community called a parish. The leader of the parish community is normally a priest. In some parts of the world, where there is a shortage of priests, it may well be led by a senior lay person or a deacon. In these circumstances a priest will visit at regular intervals to say Mass, anoint the sick and celebrate other sacraments and ceremonies.

FOR INTEREST

There are four main kinds of religious order in the Catholic Church:

- monastic: monks or nuns who live and work at their monastery and recite the daily Office of Prayers
- mendicant: friars – these may be priests or lay brothers and nuns, who live and pray together but depend on alms (charitable donations) for their livelihood
- canons regular: these are canons and canonesses who sing services and may run parishes
- clerks regular: priests who are also members of an avowed religious order and who play a more active role in secular life.

The best known of the religious orders are: Augustinians, Carmelites, Dominicans, Franciscans, Jesuits, Salesians, and the Missionary Oblates of Mary Immaculate.

There are also religious congregations, which are communities that take simple vows and are therefore not bound to an order in the same way as others.

Catholicism in the faith community and the family

The next two pages will help you to:

- develop your knowledge of how Christian communities are formed
- explore the ways in which Christian communities function
- evaluate the advantages and disadvantages of living in a Christian community.

Catholics worshipping together as a community.

A model Christian community

The early Church is a good example of a community. It was made up of the twelve apostles, with Barnabus replacing Judas, and other followers, or disciples. The community of apostles:

- shared everything they had in common
- lived together
- worshipped in each other's houses
- owned everything in common and distributed the resources to those people who were in need.

AO1 skills ACTIVITIES

Explain how and why people at the time chose to follow Jesus. Give reasons why people continue to follow him today.

The unity that is seen in this community comes from the guiding principle, 'love one another just as I have loved you,' one of Jesus' best known sayings. The love that they shared is often referred to as *agape* and is specifically meant as love among members of a group. Jesus also talked about his brothers and sisters, meaning everyone in his community. Catholics today refer to the brotherhood or sisterhood of the Church. The Church is often talked of as a family and it comes from this idea.

The early Christian community

In John's gospel, Jesus tells his beloved disciple to take Mary, his mother, back to his home and to look after her. It was this home that became the centre of the early Church and gives the model for all Catholic families. At the time, the apostles and disciples were at great risk of persecution and needed to stay close for protection and comfort. This was a group that had chosen to abandon their homes and families and follow Jesus. They were all bereaved and shocked at his death and needed each other.

The tasks of the apostles

Those who followed Jesus were asked to carry out these important tasks:

- spread his name to all the nations by preaching his message
- baptise in his name
- suffer and die for the sake of the faith.

The accounts of the travels of, for example, St Peter and St Paul, are filled with stories of their courage and determination. They also show how much rejoicing there was in the early community when they returned home, back to the early Christian family. Their brothers and sisters would have understood how much they had suffered and how much their lives were in danger. Those left behind would have prayed each day for the protection of the Holy Spirit and that God would be with them on their journeys.

MUST THINK ABOUT!

Most of the early community that was made up of the followers of Jesus were martyred for their faith. Stephen was stoned to death and tradition says that Peter was executed upside down and Andrew on a diagonal cross. Today, there are many who choose to put their lives at risk for their faith in parts of the world less safe than the United Kingdom. What things would cause you to risk your life?

AO2 skills **ACTIVITIES**

To some, Jesus said, 'Leave all and follow me.' To others Jesus said, 'Go back and tell your neighbours about me.' Compare and contrast these different ways of serving Jesus.

If following the teachings of Jesus were a criminal offence, what evidence could be used in court to convict his followers? Explain your choices and assess the strengths and challenges of being obvious and explicit about your faith.

Religious communities

The next two pages will help you to:

- identify the main types of religious communities within Catholicism
- examine the characteristics of Catholic religious communities
- demonstrate your understanding of the role of communities in spreading Jesus' message.

Many Christian religious communities are self-supporting.

Parishes and dioceses

Most Protestant and Catholic Churches are organised into local **parishes**. The size of each parish will depend on the local population, so cities like Liverpool have a large number of parishes whereas somewhere like East Anglia only has a few. Normally the person who leads the parish is a priest. In very busy parishes the priest will be supported by other assistant priests, called curates, or members of the **laity**. Some parishes have a Catholic primary school attached to them and all will encourage their parishioners to send their children to the Catholic secondary school that serves the local district.

The parish is usually governed by a parish council, which comprises women and men who have particular skills or gifts or who represent particular interests. The council takes responsibility for the funds that it needs to run the parish. It will ensure that the priests are adequately housed and that all the property the parish owns is maintained to a high standard. Some Catholic parishes also have a liturgy committee which plans the ways in which Masses and other ceremonies are celebrated.

AO1 skills ACTIVITIES

All members of religious orders take vows. Identify what they are and explain the reasons for and the value of taking them.

Many Catholic parishes also employ a sister (nun) who shares responsibility with the priests for special duties. They may:

- take Holy Communion to the sick, elderly or housebound
- lead prayer services or other acts of worship
- lead education programmes in the parish for the Sacraments of **Baptism**, **Confirmation** or the Eucharist
- act as chaplains in the local school.

Parishes are organised in regional groups called dioceses. The head of a diocese is the Bishop, with a cathedral as the centre of the diocese.

Monastic and communities of sisters

In the past, religious brothers and sisters tended to live in monasteries, convents, priories, abbeys or community houses spread throughout the population. These communities were all founded to provide opportunities for women and men to act as **disciples**. Each founder established their order in keeping with their interpretation of what Jesus wanted from the Church and their analysis of what had happened in the early Church.

There are two main types of **religious order**:

- contemplative – those committed to praying 'for the conversion of the world', such as St Teresa of Ávila
- Apostolic – those who work to convert others, such as St Francis Xavier

Any person joining a religious order will usually take three vows, which are often summarised as poverty, chastity and obedience. It is usual for a member of a religious community to promise to obey the head of their community, the abbot, the mother superior or the prior.

Benedictines, Carmelites and Franciscans

Modelling themselves on the hermits who inhabited deserted regions of the world and believed they could get close to God by stripping away all human comforts, the Benedictines were founded by St Benedict of Nursia. St Simon Stock founded the Carmelite order, modelled on the hermits and monks who lived on Mount Carmel. St Francis founded his great order, the Franciscans, on the principle that they should live as simply as Jesus did, possessing only one tunic, a pair of sandals, a staff and a small bag to carry a tiny number of possessions.

Most of these orders depended for money on their own hard work: farming, fishing, wine-making and other forms of brewing and distilling. Others survived by begging – these monks were called 'mendicants'. This comes from the Latin word meaning 'begging'. In more recent times, monks, friars and sisters have tended to earn their living working in schools, hospitals or social services.

There are still many members of religious orders who earn their place in the world by working in missionary service.

FOR DEBATE

The Vow of Poverty means giving away all personal possessions for the benefit of the community. Chastity means giving up the right to marriage and sexual relationships. Obedience means living by the commandments of the Church, the teachings of Jesus and the will of the community's 'superior'. Discuss in groups what you think about these vows.

MUST THINK ABOUT!

Consider the number of place names in England that come from the monastic communities that once existed there: Covent Garden (from the convent garden that was once there), Blackfriars Bridge, Whitefriars Street, Waltham Abbey – and these are just from the London area.

AO2 skills ACTIVITIES

Recent research suggests that members of religious communities live longer than other people. Discuss why this might be, and whether you feel living longer is worth the sacrifices.

St Francis instructed his friars to go out and preach the gospel and 'use words if you have to'. Explore other ways of preaching the gospel and assess their effectiveness.

The domestic Church

The next two pages will help you to:

- explore how Catholics express their faith as a family
- identify forms of worship that occur in Catholic homes
- evaluate the effectiveness of homes as domestic churches.

A family saying grace before they eat.

The Holy Family of Nazareth

Not much is known about Jesus' early life but St Luke gives a glimpse into the strong relationship he had with Mary, his mother, and her husband, Joseph. So dedicated was Joseph to the care of Mary and Jesus that he took them to Egypt to escape the persecution of King Herod. Later he rejoiced when he found Jesus in the temple among the elders of the Jewish faith.

The distance from Nazareth to Jerusalem is considerable. Joseph's journey shows his commitment to his family and its religious customs. Catholic families are like this and often go to extraordinary lengths to celebrate public and private acts of worship with their children. They also practise a number of rituals within their homes such as:

- saying grace before meals
- saying prayers before bedtime
- reciting the rosary together
- blessing themselves with water as they enter the front door, or when departing.

Other Christian denominations also practise some of these rituals.

AO1 skills ACTIVITIES

Create an ideas map centred on the word 'home'. Include all the religious activities which take place in the home of a practising Catholic.

It is often possible to 'tell' a Catholic home. Some of the religious objects or artefacts that might be found inside are:

- holy water stoups by the front door
- crucifixes or crosses on the walls
- small shrines to particular saints or devotions
- religious art or statues.

Advent calendars, wreaths or candles are often found in Catholic homes, as well as many other Christian homes, in December.

The characteristics of Catholic homes

Artefacts and religious objects do not make a Catholic home. What matters more is the quality of the relationships between the members of the family. Devout Catholics try to stick to a number of rules connected with family life. For example, the Catholic Church sees marriage as the most important human relationship and forbids remarriage after divorce among its members. The Catholic Church teaches that sex should only occur between a married couple and should be open to the possibility of a new life being created. For this reason the Church is against sex outside marriage, the use of artificial contraceptives and same gender relationships.

Love and forgiveness at home

Jesus' home was filled with love, and Catholic families try to ensure that their homes are similarly warm, comforting places where each member feels valued and trusted. Forgiveness is often a strong characteristic within such families because there is an acceptance that there will be times when individual members of the family fall short of the ideal. Like the story of the Lost (Prodigal) Son (see Luke Chapter 15), there is great rejoicing when someone whose behaviour may have caused offence, realises their error, apologises and has their place in the family restored.

Positive parental role models

Along with many other people, Catholics believe in the importance of the roles played by both the father and the mother in a family. In the 21st century, the edges between these roles have become more blurred than at any other time in history. What remains constant is the need for children to have positive role models so that they can grow into mature and balanced adults. Catholic beliefs are very clear about parenting, reflecting their view that God is the model father and Mary the model mother.

REMEMBER THIS

The rules of the Church are controlled by priests with special training called Canon Lawyers. Canon Law governs the whole of Catholic life from domestic relations to the laws that control how Mass should be said. When things go wrong, Catholics sometimes have to attend a tribunal run by Canon Lawyers in order to sort the matter out. Witnesses at tribunals are required to promise confidentiality and to swear an oath on a Catholic version of the Bible, in order to preserve the solemnity and dignity of the occasion.

RESEARCH NOTE

Go back to the work you did on the Lord's Prayer (see Topic 4.7). What characteristics of God are revealed in this prayer? In what ways do modern fathers resemble this model of fatherhood? Make some notes on this in your book or folder.

AO2 skills ACTIVITIES

The home is considered to be a sacred or holy place by Catholics. Work in small groups to prepare an assembly for Year 7 students to help them understand what this means.

Assess the importance of practising the faith in the home. Consider in your arguments whether parents are burdening or blessing their children when they try to pass on their beliefs.

The role of the family

The next two pages will help you to:

- identify the times when Catholic families have special celebrations
- explain the relationship between a special celebration and the stage of a person's life that it marks
- reflect on occasions when you have experienced celebrations in your own life at special times.

This first communion service is being held outside the church.

Birth, christening and first sacraments

For many families the arrival of a new child is a time for great rejoicing. In Catholic families, members of the family will pray that all goes well as the mother is about to give birth. Special prayers will be said to welcome the newborn baby, and a priest may be asked to bless the baby. At some point, the family will take the baby to church to have it christened, which is a form of **baptism** for infants.

AO1 skills ACTIVITIES

Make a list of the times and events in family life that offer opportunities for prayer and worship. These may not always be happy occasions. Share your ideas.

It is customary for **christenings** to end with a party at which the parents and godparents will celebrate the welcoming into the Church of their new son or daughter. Some of the wider family will join the party, and friends are welcomed too. There is often a christening cake and someone might propose a toast to the parents and the child. It is also normal for gifts to be given to the parents, which they look after until the child is able to look after them for themselves.

Around the age of seven, Catholic children are prepared for their first Sacrament of Reconciliation and Communion. Parents and members of the wider Church family help the child to understand why they are taking part in these rituals. Other members of the wider family may join to celebrate Holy Communion on the day it takes place. Many will pray for the child at this time. The same is true when the child reaches that time of its life when it wishes to make an adult decision about continuing in faith and celebrates the Sacrament of **Confirmation**.

Prayers and celebrations

The most visible experience of families praying together, both in public and in private, is when a person's life is coming to an end. As an elderly or sick person is dying, the family will gather around the bedside and use prayers to comfort them and also to find comfort for themselves.

After each celebration, there is usually a party at the home of the person. Even after a person has died it is traditional in some cultures to have, what is called a 'wake'. Here the family and friends will sit around the coffin and tell stories about the life of the person, sing songs and pray together for the 'repose of the soul' of the deceased (see Topic 1.8).

Mark 5:38–39

So they came to the house of the president of the synagogue, and Jesus noticed all the commotion, with people weeping and wailing unrestrainedly. He went in and said to them, 'Why all this commotion and crying? The child is not dead, but asleep.'

Communion for children

One way of looking at Communion is that it is an earthly expression of the eternal banquet that all join in when they get to Heaven. This stage in a Catholic's life is sometimes marked by having a really good party. In some **parishes** the children will join together for a 'Communion Breakfast'.

FOR INTEREST

The term 'repose of the soul' is used by Catholics as a way of describing what happens to a person after death. Catholics believe that the soul of the person is reunited with all other souls who have completed their earthly life and the prayer of those left behind is that this latest person 'going home' achieves eternal rest in Heaven.

AO2 skills ACTIVITIES

Your parents insist on saying grace before meals. You become embarrassed when friends visit. Script a conversation with your parents to discourage them and another to your friend to explain and defend your parents' behaviour.

'Catholic families are no different from any other type of family.' Consider whether or not this statement is true. Draw up a chart to show the arguments for and against this statement.

MUST THINK ABOUT!

The term 'Communion Breakfast' refers back to a time when Catholics had to fast (go without food) from midnight before making their Communion so that they were ready to receive Jesus inside them. Breaking the fast was the act of eating something in the morning. By the time the First Communion ceremony was over the children would be very hungry and would therefore have something to eat as soon as possible.

Charity and the common good

The next two pages will help you to:

- understand Catholic teachings about charity and concern for others
- know why Catholics behave in particular ways
- explain the influence of Catholic beliefs on moral practices
- demonstrate some of your beliefs that affect the way you behave.

The dignity of the human person

Catholic moral behaviour is influenced by religious beliefs and practices. For example, Catholics believe that marriage is for life, that all sexual activity should be open to the possibility of new life, and that medicine and medical technology should be used to preserve life at all costs. These moral beliefs spring from the Church's belief in the dignity of the human person and that it should be safeguarded at all times.

As a consequence of this important belief, the Church also encourages its members to promote and protect human rights. In parts of the world where human rights are in danger from political, civil or religious authorities, the Church campaigns alongside groups like Amnesty International and Human Rights Watch to ensure the freedom and safety of people. Many Catholic families support this work by giving to relevant charities, by shopping with groups like Traidcraft or purchasing Fairtrade products, or by political activism and campaigning.

Catholics believe that good moral behaviour, like charity, should begin at home. The source of Catholic moral teaching is the Ten Commandments of Moses. This template for good living includes respecting your parents, telling the truth, respecting other people's property and conducting selfless relationships, not selfish ones.

AO1 skills ACTIVITIES

Discuss the word 'family' with your work partner. Create an ideas map, using colour, symbols and key words. Include sections on the different types of relationships and the highs and lows of family living.

Family living

For many Catholics, morality can be doing things that bring peace, justice and fairness to the world and avoiding behaviours that do not. This is a simple truth and can be applied in the home as well as to situations on a worldwide scale. Like many people, Catholics try to:

- treat their children equally
- share their resources evenly
- punish bad behaviour fairly
- resolve disputes peacefully.

The word 'love' captures all these different aspects of family living. It was the word used by Jesus most frequently to describe the relationships he wanted between people.

Catholics protesting against civil partnerships.

Charity

Christianity teaches that everyone who loves God has a responsibility to care for the poor. This includes everyone, whether they are living in the next street or in a distant country. Jesus set an example of helping the poor, sick, needy and outcasts of society. He used parables to teach people how they should treat others. One of his most important teachings is in the parable of the Sheep and the Goats (Matthew 25:31–46) where, at the Last Judgement, people are judged according to whether they helped those in need or not. Those who helped the poor will be chosen for heaven.

Jesus gives examples of who the needy are and how they can be helped:

- the hungry are fed
- the thirsty are given water
- strangers are welcomed
- the naked are clothed
- the sick are cared for
- people in prison are visited.

Jesus goes on to identify himself with the poor and needy, saying that in helping them people have helped him: 'Truly I say to you, as you did it to one of the least of these my brothers, you did it to me' (Matthew 25:40b).

The sacred texts are a guide to Catholics about charity and how they should treat other people.

In an enlightening passage of the Pastoral Constitution *Gaudium et Spes*, the Second Vatican Council teaches:

> ***"When we have spread on earth the fruits of our nature and our enterprise – human dignity, fraternal communion, and freedom – according to the command of the Lord and in his Spirit, we will find them once again, cleansed this time from the stain of sin, illumined and transfigured, when Christ presents to his Father an eternal and universal kingdom... here on earth that kingdom is already present in mystery."***
>
> *Sollicitudo rei socialis* (On Social Concern) §48 (1987)

The Good Samaritan

One of the best-known stories Jesus told was about the Good Samaritan. This man acted selflessly for another who was suffering, even though his actions put him potentially in danger himself. It is a story about a man who was able to help because he had resources available, due to his own hard work. It is said that he put them to the common good.

FOR DEBATE

Have a class debate on this motion: 'Catholics have been far too concerned about the rights of the unborn child and not concerned enough with the rights of those people already living.' You will need to choose two people to speak for the motion and two to speak against it. As a class, select someone to chair the debate. You might want to record the event for the school's website.

Luke 3:11

Anyone who has two tunics must share with the one who has none, and anyone with something to eat must do the same.

James 2:14–17

How does it help, my brothers, when someone who has never done a single good act claims to have faith? Will that faith bring salvation? If one of the brothers or one of the sisters is in need of clothes and has not enough food to live on, and one of you says to them, 'I wish you well; keep yourself warm and eat plenty,' without giving them these bare necessities of life, then what good is that? In the same way faith, if good deeds do not go with it, is quite dead.

AO2 skills ACTIVITIES

Assess whether or not you have to be religious to be a good moral person. Give examples with reasons.

Explore how a Catholic family might resolve the problem of two teenagers wishing to go on a skiing trip with only enough money for one. What religious principles might inform the parents' decision and the children's response to it?

Baptism

The four signs in the Sacrament of Baptism

In Topic 5.4, you read about the form of baptism known as **christening**. It is important to know that **baptism**, whilst being a celebration of a new member of the family, is also one of the seven sacraments.

The next two pages will help you to:

- consider the important beliefs that underpin the practice of baptism
- explain the reasons why baptism is a sacrament
- evaluate the advantages of being baptised as a Catholic.

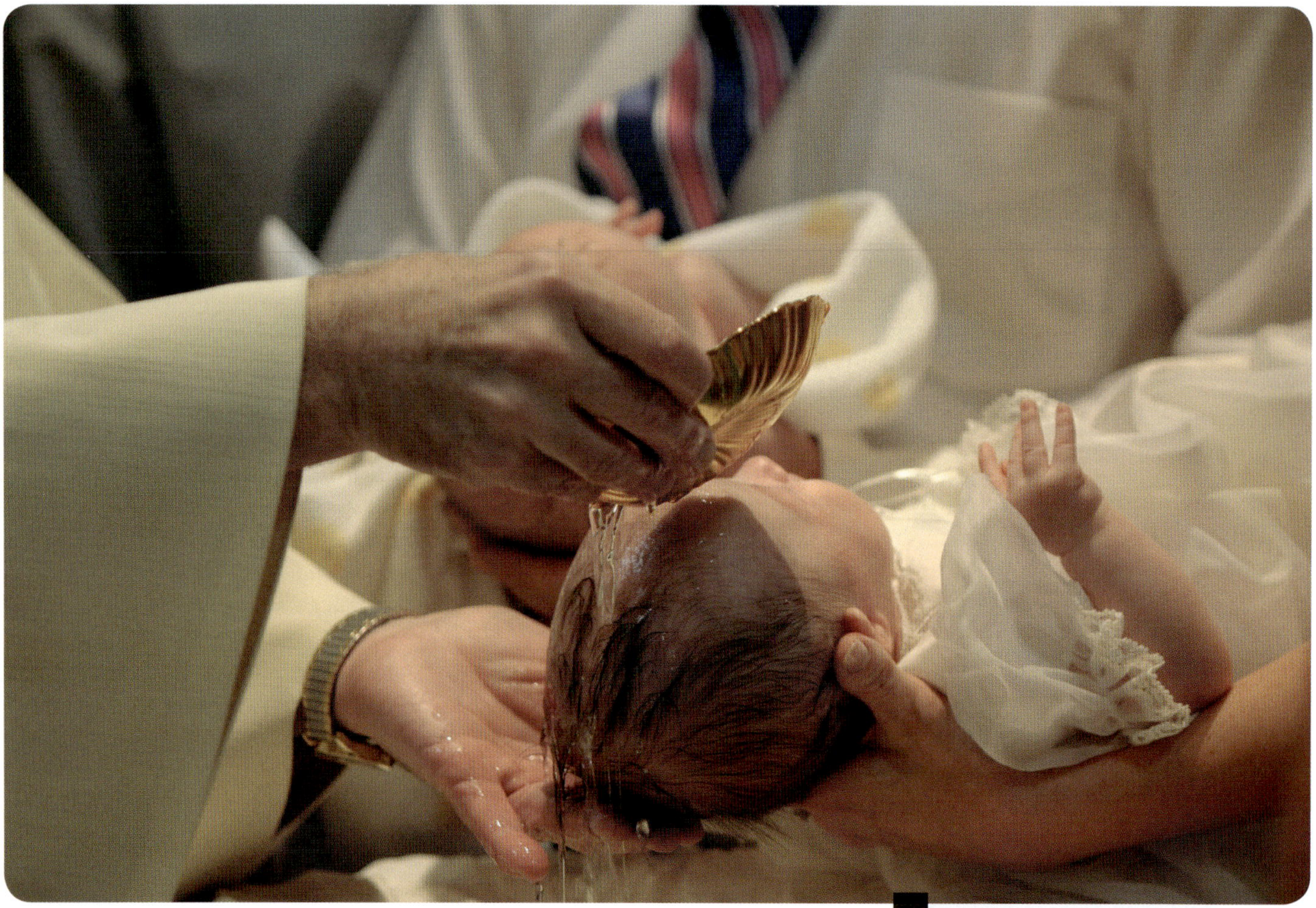

A Catholic baby being baptised.

REMEMBER THIS

'A Sacrament is an outward visible sign of an inward invisible grace.' This statement is a reminder that religious events are often made real through the use of signs and symbols. In the case of baptism, what is being symbolised is the transmission of grace (blessing) from God to people. The person receiving the sacrament experiences a change internally, even if they cannot feel it, while everyone outside witnesses it occurring through the actions of the priest or other minister.

AO1 skills ACTIVITIES

Describe and explain, with illustrations, all the qualities, interests and wisdom you would like to pass on to your children.

There are four important signs in the Sacrament of Baptism, which represent important changes to the person being baptised, as shown in the table.

Physical action	Symbolic meaning
Pouring of water or immersion in water	Infants are baptised by the priest pouring water on to their heads three times to represent the Trinity. Adult Catholics can be baptised by total immersion in water to symbolise the purification of their soul, in the way that John baptised Jesus in the River Jordan. It is still common for adults to be baptised using water poured from a jug. Sometimes this is water that has come from the River Jordan or another place of pilgrimage such as Lourdes.
Anointing with chrism	Each person being baptised is anointed with two types of oil (chrism and catechumens) which are usually applied in the 'sign of the cross'. They represent different things (naming and strengthening) but both symbolise the special benefits of joining the Church.
Clothing in a white garment	The baptised person is symbolically wrapped in a white garment as a symbol of the purification of their soul that has occurred through the cleansing action of the priest. One of the important things that Catholics believe happens in baptism is the removal of the stain of original sin. The white garment symbolises this purification. (The colour white is also used in Catholicism to symbolise the purity of a bride on her wedding day, the peace brought by a dove and the resurrection of Jesus on Easter Sunday.)
Presentation of a candle	Jesus said, 'I am the light of the world.' This is symbolised by the godparents holding a lighted candle during the baptism. The candle represents Jesus and is usually lit from the Paschal candle, which is itself ignited from a bonfire lit during the Easter vigil. That candle is dipped in the holy water that is used in baptisms. In the past, many new converts to Catholicism were baptised during the Easter vigil, while other members of the congregation take the opportunity to renew their baptismal vows. All of this shows the relationship between the suffering, death and resurrection of Jesus and the new life given to members of the Church.

MUST THINK ABOUT!

The idea of original sin can be a problem for Catholics because it comes from a time when they thought the Bible was literally true. In Genesis, Adam sinned and was thrown out of the Garden of Eden. This was the original sin. Because people believed that Adam was the first man, they reasoned that sin was an inherited characteristic – rather like DNA for bad behaviour.

In order to make up for Adam's sin someone had to break the power of death, something that only God could do. So, Jesus – who was God, as Catholics believe – came to Earth to 'redeem' humankind. Symbolically the original sin is washed away in baptism, which gives each person the chance to live an eternal life back in paradise – a state of grace. Catholics still sin, even if they have been baptised, but they redeem their own sins, when they are old enough, by receiving the Sacrament of Reconciliation (see Topic 4.7).

Infant and adult baptism

In some other Christian traditions, the decision to be baptised and join the Church is taken by an adult. Catholic families take this decision for their children because they fear that a person who dies unbaptised would not be in a state of grace and could not, therefore, go to Heaven. It is important to remember that baptism has this dual purpose: to welcome a new member into the Church and to ensure the person's pathway to Heaven.

FOR DEBATE

Discuss whether parents should baptise their children or wait until they are old enough to decide for themselves.

The marriage ceremony

The next two pages will help you to:

- explain why Catholics see marriage as the most important human relationship
- identify the important elements of a Catholic marriage ceremony
- evaluate your own attitudes to marriage and how they might affect your own life choices.

A Catholic marriage ceremony.

Christian marriage

For Christians and members of many other faiths, the ceremony of **matrimony** or marriage is an outward sign of the union of a woman and a man. All marriage ceremonies are full of symbolism, and some of the symbols are shared across different faiths. The symbolism seen in Catholic marriage includes:

- the bride wears white as a symbol of purity
- the rings that the couple exchange are signs that their relationship is never-ending
- the joining of the hands of the couple symbolises their coming together as wife and husband
- the signing of the register is a public sign of their new status as a married couple
- the vows that they exchange are a sign of the promises they make to each other
- sexual intercourse is a physical sign of the joining of a couple in holy matrimony.

AO1 skills ACTIVITIES

Make an acrostic using the word 'matrimony'. Illustrate your page with symbols from the marriage service.

The characteristics of Christian marriage

Christian marriages have a number of key characteristics:

- exclusivity
- permanence
- maturity.

Exclusivity

'Exclusivity' means that the couple will be faithful to each other. Catholics believe that a married couple should only have one sexual partner, their husband or wife. The benefit of this is that they are more likely to have a stable relationship full of trust and mutual respect. Being exclusive in a marriage avoids all sorts of complications, but it requires tremendous commitment and hard work.

Permanence

'Permanence' means that the couple will remain together until death finally separates them. Most Catholics believe that, after death, they will be reunited with their loved one in Heaven. The permanence of a married relationship will bring security and stability to any children who are born to the couple.

Maturity

'Maturity' means that the marriage relationship will help give people those things they need to develop as mature and balanced adults. People grow and develop differently but there is a lot of evidence to suggest that life-affirming relationships built on mutual trust and respect are very important for a healthy society.

The bride of Christ

In the Old Testament, the relationship that God had with his people was likened to the relationship of a married couple. Indeed the Church sometimes describes itself as the 'bride of Christ'. The kind of love that is required to keep this relationship going is a mixture of sexual love, which is essential for the continuation of the human race, and a deeper, more spiritual, love that is about a coming together of two different people into one united whole.

Nuptial Mass

Many Catholics choose to get married at a Nuptial Mass. It sets a context for the relationship and gives their family, friends and the local community the chance to pray for special blessings to come to them as a married couple. In addition to the exchange of vows, the priest or minister will also recite a number of prayers which focus on the specific roles each partner will take in the relationship.

The decision to commit to someone for the rest of your life is a massive one. It is a huge step, which requires lots of support. The marriage ceremony is only the formal beginning of the relationship, but it is right that it should be taken very seriously and celebrated in a special way. The couple may choose favourite readings, pieces of music, types and colours of flowers and they may even write their own vows.

MUST THINK ABOUT!

Imagine you were to write a lonely hearts advert for a local newspaper, looking for a potential marriage partner. What qualities would you ask the person to have? What physical characteristics would you want? Would it matter what your friends thought of the person?

AO2 skills ACTIVITIES

Analyse the reasons why some people believe that living together is just the same as being married. Assess the strengths and weaknesses of this argument.

Sit in small groups in a circle. In turn, go round the circle with everyone giving a reason why marriage should last until death and then why it should not. Share the best of the reasons with the rest of the class and prepare a class debate.

Topic 5.8

Ordination and the consecration of priests

The next two pages will help you to:

- describe what happens at an ordination
- explain the reasons for a celibate clergy in the Catholic Church
- make an informed judgement about the teachings of the Church in relation to holy orders.

Catholic priests are ordained by a bishop.

Becoming a priest

Catholic priests are able to do two things that lay people cannot do:

- give absolution during the Sacrament of Reconciliation
- consecrate the bread and wine during Eucharist to make it holy and to make Jesus really present.

These are special powers given to them during their **ordination**. Ordination is a special ceremony that is conducted by a bishop. To prepare for ordination, priests have to go through a long process of education and training. They have to commit to a celibate lifestyle which, on paper, means not ever marrying, but in reality is a promise to abstain from sexual relationships. The intention of this rule of the Church is to make priests available for the service of their people at any hour of the day.

Priests also promise to obey their bishop and to go where they are sent. This is the same as the command given to the **apostles** by Jesus. They also promise to give all their possessions away and to live a simple life in the service of the Church.

AO1 skills ACTIVITIES

A priest is expected to be both a 'servant' and a 'shepherd' to his congregation. Think about these two words. Explain how a present-day priest might put these ideas into practice.

The person preparing for the priesthood is called an 'ordinand'. The ordination ceremony can be conducted in the ordinand's home **parish**, the parish where they are going to serve the early years of their ministry, or at a place of worship which is special to them. In the ceremony, the ordinand makes a public statement of his faith and of his intentions to become a priest. As a sign of obedience and humility he prostrates himself (lies flat on his face) in front of the altar and the bishop 'lays hands' on him. This is another reminder of Jesus' act of commissioning his apostles.

Mark 3:13–15

He now went up onto the mountain and summoned those he wanted. So they came to him and he appointed twelve; they were to be his companions and to be sent out to proclaim the message, with power to drive out devils.

Becoming a nun

The early Christian community contained a number of women who carried out important roles. Mary, Jesus' mother, received his body from the cross. Mary of Magdala was the first person to whom Jesus appeared after the resurrection, and there were others who are mentioned in the scriptures. It is important, therefore, that women's ministry in the Church is recognised.

Women cannot be priests because the Church teaches that priests represent Jesus, who was a man. Many other Christian denominations allow women to be priests or to minister to or serve the congregation. Women who wish to serve God often live out this vocation (calling) by joining a **religious order**. Like priests, they go through a series of special ceremonies where they profess their faith and the vows of their order. There are usually vows of poverty, chastity and obedience.

Becoming a bishop

A bishop is the head of a region, or diocese, of the Church. Bishops are consecrated for their role by the Pope. The consecration ceremony often takes place in Rome and is witnessed by other senior members of the Church. Bishops are appointed, not elected or selected through an application process. They have to be skilled in theology, politics and finance because their role will often bring them into contact with building programmes (schools and churches) as well as ministering to their flock. Bishops always have a Cathedral and there are some famous Catholic cathedrals in England, such as Liverpool and Westminster.

In every cathedral there is a large throne which belongs to the bishop. The word 'cathedral' means 'throne' and it is the place where he sits to govern his people. When the Pope, who is Bishop of Rome, sits on his throne and makes a statement, special significance is attached to it. He is speaking *ex cathedra* – literally, out of his throne – and what he says cannot be wrong.

MUST THINK ABOUT!

Bishop comes from the Greek word '*episcopos*' meaning 'overseer'. The first overseer within the Church was St Peter, which is why the Basilica in Rome, said to be built over St Peter's tomb, is the most important place of worship in Catholicism. Priests are sent out by the bishop to do God's work.

AO2 skills ACTIVITIES

Catholic priests are expected to be both male and celibate. What arguments could you put forward to defend and oppose these positions?

The shortage of priests to celebrate Mass and the other sacraments is becoming a real problem. Discuss the possible reasons for the shortage and draw up an action plan to try to resolve the situation.

The Sacrament of Anointing the Sick

The next two pages will help you to:

- explore the ceremonies that Catholics experience when they are suffering
- explain the comfort that Catholics experience from taking the Sacrament of the Sick
- form your own opinion about the value of receiving sacraments to provide comfort.

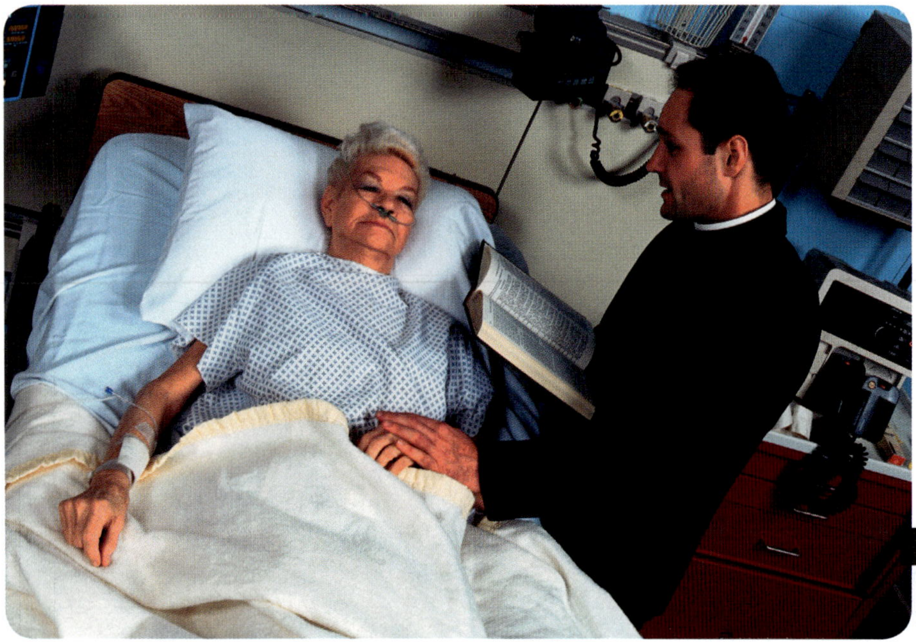

A Catholic priest with a sick person in hospital.

AO1 skills ACTIVITIES

Catholics believe that the Sacrament of the Sick can always heal, even if not cure, the sick. Explain the difference between healing and curing, with examples.

Jesus and healing

In Biblical stories of miracles, Jesus cured or healed many people during his time on earth. Now, modern medicine and science can help people to recover from cancer and to overcome mental health problems, and people can be nurtured back to life when death threatens from many types of illness. Suffering, pain and death are part of the human condition and Catholics understand this very well. Some Catholics believe that accepting pain or suffering in their life is a way of praising God for the gift of salvation. Some martyrs and other holy people even tempted pain and death as a way of showing their love of God.

Praying for healing

Prayers are always offered at Mass for the sick and dying in a **parish** or other Catholic community. There is usually one bidding prayer on a Sunday for those who have died and it is common to pray for the dead on their anniversary. Some families will gather round the grave of a person who has died in order to pray for the 'repose of the soul'.

MUST THINK ABOUT!

Consider a time when someone you knew, loved or cared about died. What was the effect on those around them? How did people show their feelings? What ceremonies or rituals took place to mark their death? For whose benefit do you think these events occurred, the dead person or those they left behind?

It is often said that the only happy person at a funeral is the person who has died. In many ways the ceremony itself provides comfort for the family since, according to Catholic belief, the deceased is on her or his way to Heaven. The Sacrament of the Sick is different. It takes place before the person dies, so it acts as a way of:

- preparing them for the future life they are about to experience
- providing comfort for them at a troubling, sometimes painful and often frightening time
- giving them an opportunity to make public their desire to spend eternity with God.

The Sacrament of the Sick

In the past, it was common to hear people calling 'Fetch the priest' when someone was about to die. This was because Catholics believed that a person had to die 'in a state of grace' if they wanted to go to Heaven. The priest would anoint the person, hear their last confession – if they could speak – and give them Holy Communion. This ritual has a technical name *'viaticum'* which can be taken to mean 'send them on their way'. Often this was referred to as 'The Last Rites', because it was the last thing that a person experienced in their life.

Today, the ritual is more widely known as the Sacrament of the Sick and is an outward sign, through gestures and words, of a special blessing (grace) that is being given to a disabled, sick or dying person.

The power of touch

The 'laying on of hands' is a symbolic way of communicating the healing power to the sick or dying person. Jesus was seen doing this on many occasions. Such was his healing power that many people believed they could be cured simply by touching the hem of his cloak.

Tradition says that Mary of Magdala soothed Jesus by anointing him with ointment when he was weary and probably scared about what was to happen to him. She used a lotion called 'nard', which was used in ancient medicine and healing techniques. The use of oils of anointment in the Sacrament of the Sick reminds Catholics of this action.

Mark 14:3

He was at Bethany in the house of Simon, a man who had suffered from a virulent skin-disease; he was at table when a woman came in with an alabaster jar of very costly ointment, pure nard. She broke the jar and poured the ointment on his head.

Mark 8:23

He took the blind man by the hand and led him outside the village. Then, putting spittle on his eyes and laying his hands on him, he asked, 'Can you see anything?'

MUST THINK ABOUT!

What do physiotherapy and Jesus have in common? Physiotherapists are trained to make damaged muscles and bones recover. They use physical manipulation, massage and other techniques like hydrotherapy and heat treatment to do their work. In some cases they will use creams, lotions or other chemicals. The Sacrament of the Sick is a symbolic way of offering physical healing like this within Catholicism.

AO2 skills ACTIVITIES

'Physical suffering should be endured and offered up' used to be a common way of thinking for Catholics. Assess the value of this way of approaching life's difficulties, especially illness.

Cardinal John Henry Newman once wrote that even in our sickness we can usefully serve the Lord. Catholics saw how true this was in the last years of Pope John Paul II's illness. Examine what it means to serve God when you are ill, elderly or dying.

The importance of the Catholic faith in the wider community

The next two pages will help you to:

- identify important Catholic figures within the wider community
- assess the contribution of Catholics to public life
- evaluate whether Catholic beliefs and values make an important contribution to public life.

When he resigned as Prime Minister of Great Britain, Tony Blair decided to convert to Catholicism.

A01 skills ACTIVITIES

Working with a partner, make a list of ten people who you think are famous. Now, for each one, explain why you have chosen them. Look at your responses. Would you now change your list and why?

Famous Catholics

Even when he was the Prime Minister of Great Britain, Tony Blair was seen going to Mass with his family. Underpinning many of Tony Blair's actions in politics, and since he ceased to be Prime Minister, were firmly held beliefs, many of which stem from his Christian faith.

Since leaving his job he has converted to Catholicism. You can read more about this on the Tony Blair Faith Foundation website.

Other famous people who were or are clear about their Catholic faith are Anne Widdecombe MP, Ruth Kelly MP, actor Mel Gibson and former US President John F. Kennedy. These people have all acted in accordance with their beliefs and would say that they have tried to make the world a better place by so doing.

Catholicism in the global community

Pictured with Tony Blair is the present Pope, Benedict XVI. His predecessor Pope John Paul II was a very influential international figure at the end of the 20th century. Karol Józef Wojtyła, to give him his Polish name, was the first non-Italian Pope for hundreds of years. When he became Pope, Poland was one of many countries controlled by the former Soviet Union, which was anti-religious. The election of Wojtyła to the papacy gave a huge boost to Polish campaigners for independence.

The break with Communist rule came with the election of the former trade union leader Lech Wałesa as President of Poland in 1990. This event was part of a wave of peaceful transitions from Soviet control, with numerous central European nations previously governed by Moscow becoming independent and free.

Catholic communities all over the UK have been enriched in recent years by the influx of young migrants from countries like Poland, Lithuania and the Ukraine who became free to travel once the yoke of Soviet oppression was lifted.

Catholics in the local community

The Pope is the head of a very big human community, with huge influence. If it were a country it would be equivalent to the population of somewhere like India. Only a few Catholics are able to affect global events; most can only influence the world on their doorstep.

Catholic schools are an obvious sign of the Church in a local community. They are places which are characterised by:

- a strong sense of moral purpose and a clear identity
- strong systems of pastoral care
- an inclusive ethos, which recognises the diversity of backgrounds from which Catholic children come
- firm but fair discipline and an atmosphere of love, especially forgiveness.

Catholic school children will often work for the common good by:

- organising and taking part in charity events
- being considerate to the school's neighbours
- setting examples of good moral behaviour and treating others with dignity and respect
- campaigning on issues of injustice or equality.

FOR DEBATE

'Pope John Paul II was as important a person in the 20th century as Martin Luther King Jr or Mahatma Gandhi. His contribution is yet to be recognised but will be in the future.' Discuss this with your desk partner. Then share your findings with the rest of the class.

MUST THINK ABOUT!

In groups design a sales brochure for a Catholic school. What things would you feature? What would be its unique characteristics? How would it be different from other community schools?

AO2 skills ACTIVITIES

'People should always be proud of their faith and never be afraid to say what religion they are.' Do you agree with this statement? Consider what circumstances might make someone not want to say that they belonged to a particular religion. How might a Catholic respond to this statement?

GradeStudio

Welcome to the Grade Studio

GCSE is about what you can do, not what you can't do. You need to know what examiners want in your answers so that you can get the best possible marks. In GCSE Religious Studies there are two things that examiners are looking for. These are called assessment objectives (AO). Questions are designed to help examiners find out how well you do in each assessment objective.

Graded examples for this topic

AO1

AO1 questions test what you know and how well you can explain and analyse things. Let's look at an AO1 question to see what examiners are expecting you to do.

Question

Explain why Christians might support a Catholic aid agency such as CAFOD. **[6 marks]**

To reach the highest levels in your response you will need to use your knowledge of an agency and explain how its work and the reasons it gives for its work match Christian beliefs.

Level 1 The candidate will demonstrate little understanding of the question. The answer will be too simple with little or no relevant information.	Select an agency, preferably one you have studied in depth. At this level the response will outline what the agency does and why, for example CAFOD aims to provide emergency aid, short-term aid, long-term aid and education to help less fortunate people, because it follows the teaching of Jesus.
Level 2 The candidate will show some understanding of the question. Some relevant information will be included but may lack detail.	Go on to explain Christian teaching about charity and concern for others. Refer, for example, to Jesus' actions in healing the sick and his parables such as the sheep and the goats or the commandment 'love your neighbour as yourself'. Say why this relates to CAFOD.
Level 3 The candidate will show a clear understanding of the question with a fairly complete description/ explanation/analysis.	Link the work of CAFOD directly to this teaching and use any further information about the organisation to support this. For example, state that CAFOD will help all people and not just Christians, and that it aims to make people self sufficient and give them dignity. Conclude with a brief summary of how the organisation's purpose and principles match Christian attitudes and say that Catholics might support it by giving money, working for the organisation or purchasing its products.

AO2

Question

'Catholic parents should bring their children up to be Catholics.' Discuss this statement. **[12 marks]**

The response to this statement must refer to different points of view, with justification. The response will be marked by levels and the highest level will be awarded for a balanced response with your own view, supported by evidence and argument. There are four levels for AO2 responses, so let's look at the way you could structure a response to reach Level 4.

Level 1 The candidate will demonstrate little understanding of the question. The answer will be too simple with little or no relevant information.	Unpack the question so that the examiner knows you have understood the issue. The key word is 'should'. You need to think about reasons for and against parents bringing their children up in the faith. A first point could be that the parent promised to do this when the child was baptised.
Level 2 The candidate will show some understanding of the question. Some relevant information will be included but often the answer is one-sided.	Go on to develop this reason, with knowledge of the promises made at baptism, and explain how this means parents have a duty to bring their children up as Catholics. Give another view in support of this, for example that if the parents are Catholic their children will naturally be involved their Catholic lifestyle.
Level 3 The candidate will show a satisfactory understanding of the question with a range of relevant material and appropriate evidence.	Consider a different view, for example children should not be forced against their will into any religious activities. Evaluate this view by suggesting that children may not be able to make up their minds until they are older and that parents may believe that they have a right to expect their children to live according to lifestyle of the family. Give your personal view.
Level 4 The candidate will show a clear understanding of the question with a range of fully supported viewpoints backed by relevant evidence and argument.	Comment on the views expressed so far and then explain your own, which might be that Catholic parents have the duty to bring their children up in the faith, but that when they are old enough children should be given the opportunity to make up their own minds, or your view might be that it is wrong to try to influence children about religion.

These specimen answers provide an outline of how you could construct your response. Space does not allow us to give a full response. The examiner will be looking for more detail in your actual exam responses.

Remember and Reflect

AO1 Describe, explain and analyse, using knowledge and understanding

Question	Find the answer on:
1 Name three ceremonies that mark the different stages in the lives of Catholics.	PAGE 117, 129, 130
2 Explain why Catholics baptise their babies.	PAGE 129
3 Give an account of a baptism ceremony.	PAGE 124
4 What is a monastic community?	PAGE 121
5 Write down the names of the founders of these Catholic religious orders: a *Franciscans* b *Carmelites* c *Benedictines*	PAGE 117
6 Describe three of the tasks that Jesus gave to his apostles.	PAGE 117
7 What is the name given to a regional group of Catholic parishes?	PAGE 121
8 Explain the purpose of the vows that are taken by the clergy and other religious groups.	PAGE 132
9 Identify at least four things (religious objects) that would enable a stranger to tell that they were in a Catholic home.	PAGE 123
10 Explain the job of a Canon Lawyer.	PAGE 123
11 Why are special religious ceremonies often followed by a family party or meal?	PAGE 125
12 What lessons do Catholics take from the story of the Good Samaritan?	PAGE 127
13 Explain the symbolism of at least one of the oils used in baptism.	PAGE 129
14 Explain the symbolism of the white garment used to clothe a person after they have been baptised.	PAGE 129
15 Explain the symbolism of the rings at a wedding.	PAGE 130
16 What do Catholics mean by the term 'permanence' in relation to marriage?	PAGE 131
17 What benefits do Catholics believe can be gained by praying for the sick, dying and deceased?	PAGE 134–135

AO2 Use evidence and reasoned argument to express and evaluate personal responses, informed insights, and differing viewpoints

1 If you have children will you: have them baptised while they are still infants, wait until they are teenagers before baptising them, or allow them to make up their own mind about whether or not they wish to be baptised? Explain your choice.

2 Do you think children should wear their own clothes to make their first communion or continue with the custom of wearing special clothes, for example a white dress for girls? Explain your thinking.

3 What do you think of the Catholic rule that prevents women from becoming priests? Set out the reasons that underpin what you think.

4 Do you agree or disagree that the priesthood should remain a celibate occupation? What are the benefits to the Church of celibacy? What might be some of the disadvantages?

5 What, in your opinion, is the value of the ancient vows of poverty, chastity and obedience?

6 'Where I come from, when somebody dies there's a thing called a wake. Everyone comes round the house and sits by the open coffin. They have a drink and a chat, someone tells stories about the dead person and then people start to sing. They have a great time.' For many people the practice of a 'wake' is disrespectful; they think it should be a quiet time of reflection and sadness. What do you think? You can talk about your own experiences of celebrating the end of someone's life.

7 Do you think there is any point in praying for a sick person to get better?

8 Picture the family of Joseph, Mary and Jesus. Does it present an image of an ideal family? Is this an ideal that is too difficult for most families to attain? Is it an unrealistic model?

Topic 6: Sacred writings

The Big Picture

In this Topic you will be examining:

- the texts that Catholics consider to be sacred scriptures
- the place of the Bible in the canon of sacred literature
- other texts and writings that are considered holy by the Church
- different approaches to the authority of the Bible
- your own attitude to the authority of the Bible.

What?

You will:

- explore the make-up and composition of the Bible
- examine aspects of the Old and New Testaments and the apocrypha
- consider the importance of Vatican documents
- evaluate the claims to truth contained in each of these different forms of sacred writing.

Why?

Because:

- the Bible is an important source of truth for Catholics
- other sacred texts contribute to Catholics' understanding of their belief system and the way the world is
- it is important to know why Catholics have a different Bible from other Christians
- sacred texts are used frequently by Catholics trying to make sense of things that happen today.

How?

By:

- reading some important passages from the scriptures
- examining what other people have said about sacred writings
- comparing and contrasting Catholic approaches to sacred writings with those of other Christians
- reflecting on your own approach to the authority of the Bible and its claims to truth.

The lectern of the Cathedral of Notre-Dame in Chartres, created by the artist Goudji.

GET STARTED

'The Bible is irrelevant to the world today.' Do you agree or disagree? Give reasons. Do a survey to find out what people think about this question and why.

Sacred writings

The Liturgy of the word is a very important part of the Mass.

KEY INFORMATION

- Many of the world's great religions have a book, or books, that they consider to be sacred writings.
- A sacred book may contain the history of the religion, including the life of the founder and other key figures, and the main beliefs and teachings about how people should live. In Christianity, the sacred book is the Bible.
- The Bible contains different kinds of literature, including history, laws, prophecy, poetry, the gospels (accounts of Jesus' life and teachings), letters, the book of Acts (telling the story of the early Church) and Revelation (a book written to encourage Christians under persecution).
- The Bible is made up of 66 books and is divided into two parts. The first part is the Old Testament, which is made up of 39 books that were written before the time of Jesus. The second part, the New Testament, is made up of 27 books, which were written after the life of Jesus and before the end of the 2nd century CE.
- Some versions of the Bible, particularly those used by Catholics, also include some books from another collection of sacred writings known as the apocrypha.

- The Bible is important to Christians because it is a source of Christian beliefs, is a guide to life and contains the word of God.
- Many Christians believe it is the inspired word of God and is literally true.
- The Bible is used by Christians in their public and private worship.

KEY QUESTIONS

KNOWLEDGE AND UNDERSTANDING

Who wrote the Bible?

Is the Bible literally the Word of God?

Can anyone write a sacred text?

ANALYSIS AND EVALUATION

How and in what ways are sacred texts used in public worship?

How should the Bible be treated by those using it for study at GCSE level?

KEY WORDS

apocrypha Those books of the Bible that are included by Catholics but not by all Christians.

Bible Christian holy book; from the Greek word *biblos* meaning 'book' or 'library'.

canon The agreed collection of books in the Bible.

gospel One of the four books of the New Testament that relate the stories of Jesus in his life on earth.

evangelist Someone who proclaims the word of God as described in the scriptures.

lectern The stand in a church from which sacred texts are read.

lectionary A special book of the readings to be used in Mass or a book with a list of these readings.

scripture A general name for the sacred writings of Christianity and other faiths.

Testament A testament is a statement that someone has sworn is true.

translation The process by which the original words of the Bible were converted into the vernacular.

vernacular The ordinary language of the people reading the Bible.

FOR INTEREST 'Myth' comes from the Greek word '*mythos*' which means 'story'. It is now used to describe a story that has religious importance for believers. The story may or may not be true, but that does not change the truth of the teachings it contains for believers.

The Bible

The next two pages will help you to:

- examine the structure and composition of the Bible
- explain why the Bible is still widely read
- evaluate different views about the authority of the Bible.

Creating the Bible

Over the past few years, television has become dominated by reality shows such as the *X Factor* and *Strictly Come Dancing*. In each case celebrities are recreated or created anew by their willingness to present themselves and their talent to two different types of judges. On the one hand there are so-called experts like Simon Cowell, Len Goodman and Andrew Lloyd Webber; on the other hand, talent is judged by public opinion.

There have been some well-publicised cases of the public voting people out of a show or keeping them in against the judgement of the expert panel. This is because people have different opinions, perspectives and prejudices about what they are seeing or hearing.

AO1 skills **ACTIVITIES**

Describe a story or a book which has influenced you for the better. Explain how and give five reasons why it should still be read in the year 3000.

The **Bible** has come to our generation, in its present form, through a series of processes that depended on the will of some people over the opinions of others. There are a number of accounts of the life of Jesus which did not make the final edition – these are called the apocryphal **gospels**. There are other ancient writings that were not included in the Hebrew **scriptures**, known to Christians as the Old **Testament** which are known as the apocrypha or pseudepigrapha.

Some other early writings of the apostles or their followers might also have been included but were left out because they did not meet the criteria of those selecting the books that did make it. One of these people was St Irenaeus, the Bishop of Lugdunum (now Lyons), France very early in the 2nd century CE.

Jewish Torah scrolls which contain the first five books of the Bible.

The Canon of Scripture

It is important to remember that the Bible is a collection of books. Different denominations have agreed on different **canons** or collections of books. At the time of Jesus the books that made up the Hebrew scriptures were written on individual scrolls. Jesus read from the scrolls when he entered the synagogue in the towns he was visiting.

Luke 4:16–21

He went to Nazareth, where he had been brought up, and on the Sabbath day he went into the synagogue, as was his custom. And he stood up to read. The scroll of the prophet Isaiah was handed to him. Unrolling it, he found the place where it is written:
'The Spirit of the Lord is on me,
because he has anointed me
to preach good news to the poor.
He has sent me to proclaim freedom for the prisoners
and recovery of sight for the blind,
to release the oppressed,
to proclaim the year of the Lord's favour.'
Then he rolled up the scroll, gave it back to the attendant and sat down. The eyes of everyone in the synagogue were fastened on him, and he began by saying to them, 'Today this scripture is fulfilled in your hearing.'

RESEARCH NOTE

Using your class Bibles, identify which books fit into the forms of literature you have seen. Make a diagram to show this. Remember that Catholic Bibles have six books called the apocrypha, so you need to ensure you are using the full version.

Jesus was a learned man who knew the scriptures very well. The prophet Isaiah was a big influence on his preaching and mission. Isaiah was one of the Jewish prophets. The book of Isaiah and the books of other prophets can be found in the Old Testament, along with books of history, the law, poetry and wisdom.

In the New Testament, which starts with the gospels – the stories of Jesus' life on earth – there are also historical books, the letters of the early apostles and a visionary book attributed to John the Divine called Revelation.

Contemporary uses of the Bible

Jesus drew on his reading of the prophet Isaiah for inspiration. Here are some of the reasons that people have given for still reading the Bible:

- it gives me comfort in times of need
- it gives potential solutions for the problems of life
- I look for meaning and truth
- it provides wisdom
- my mum read it and I want to know why
- I wondered what all the fuss was about.

AO2 skills ACTIVITIES

Book shops still claim that the Bible is the number one bestseller. Explore the reasons why some people might own a Bible yet never read it. Examine the benefits and losses involved.

The Old Testament

The next two pages will help you to:

- analyse the Old Testament and explore its significance for Catholics today
- understand some of the key passages of the Old Testament and what they mean for Catholics today
- make judgements about the wisdom of citing the Old Testament in support of opinions, attitudes or values you might have today.

Moses and the Ten Commandments (Exodus 20).

Old Testament – the book of God?

Reading the Old **Testament** can cause some confusion. God is portrayed as a father figure and creator, as a loving shepherd who tends his flock, as a still small voice of calm and also as a jealous, wrathful and vengeful destroyer. He is reported as drowning all the Pharaoh's men, turning Lot's wife into a pillar of salt, striking down various people with thunderbolts and inspiring the Hebrews to ransack and pillage ancient cities they had conquered, like Jericho.

God appears in many guises and with many names: Yahweh, the Lord, 'I am he who is'. This is because the Old Testament was written by different people at different times as they tried to make sense of the world around them. They did this without the benefits of modern technology and the understanding humans have acquired about the way the world is.

AO1 skills ACTIVITIES

'Christians should ignore the Old Testament and only read the New Testament.' How might a Catholic react to this? What do you think? Give reasons for your answers, showing that you refer to Christian beliefs.

Old Testament parables

Catholics are used to learning that many of the stories in the New Testament are parables, which are stories with a meaning. The parables of the Sower, the Good Samaritan and the Lost Son are all good examples. The Old Testament is like this: a series of stories packed with meaning and symbols but which may not be literally true.

The story of the Exodus is one such story. It tells of the birth of the Hebrew nation and of the actions that Moses took to form a community by using wisdom he picked up from other cultures. Similar sets of rules to the Ten Commandments can be found in the records of other ancient civilisations since they make sense as rules for living.

Catholic use of the Old Testament

At every Mass, there is a reading from the Old Testament, which is normally twinned with a reading from the New Testament to make a theme for the day. It takes three years to read through the whole cycle. On Sundays and holy days, the readings are enhanced by the singing or recitation of one of the Psalms, which is also on the same theme. The readings are set out in a special book called a **lectionary**, often with a page for each day.

It is the job of the priest or preacher to interpret the **scriptures** and explain their meaning to the congregation. Some of the stories need explanation since they contain elements that we might now consider to be myths.

For example, the story of Jonah and the great fish or whale is a story about a man who was 'swallowed up' by his own selfishness and, as a result, refused to do God's work. Such was God's desire that the people of Nineveh hear his message that he went to extraordinary lengths to send his messenger to them. There are many messages that Catholics can understand in this story by reading it today.

Jonah 1:16–17

Then they took Jonah and threw him overboard, and the raging sea grew calm. At this the men greatly feared the Lord, and they offered a sacrifice to the Lord and made vows to him.

But the Lord provided a great fish to swallow Jonah, and Jonah was inside the fish three days and three nights.

MUST THINK ABOUT!

The story of the creation in the Old Testament is a powerful parable and a symbolic story. Scientists believe that the world could not have been created in six days. We know there is evidence in the natural world for a form of evolution, and science has shown that there is a necessary order for evolution to have followed. First, there needed to be light for photosynthesis, and water to support life. The first forms of life would have been plants and organic matter. Eventually, single-cell structures evolved into complex organisms like human beings.

Obviously the author of the creation story did not know any of this, but the story of the creation can be read as an early parable of evolution.

AO2 skills ACTIVITIES

The liturgy of the Mass contains readings and prayers from the Old Testament. Examine the importance of including these scripture passages for Catholic worship today.

According to scholars, some stories in the Old Testament fall into the literary category of a myth, yet for many Christians these myths are true. Analyse what is meant by the phrase 'the truth of myth', giving examples from the Old Testament.

The gospels

The four gospels

The New Testament opens with four books called **gospels**. The name comes from the Anglo-Saxon word *'godspel'* which means 'good news'. They tell the good news of Jesus' salvation.

The next two pages will help you to:

- examine the significance of the gospels for Catholics
- identify the different approaches of the gospel writers
- evaluate the use of the gospels as support for people's beliefs and attitudes.

A stained-glass window showing Jesus and the four gospel writers.

AO1 skills ACTIVITIES

The word 'gospel' means 'good news'. Describe how and explain why the first four books of the New Testament were so called.

Although the four gospels tell the story of Jesus' life, there are differences between them. The table opposite sets out different aspects and content of the four gospels. These have been deduced by scholars working on the archaeology and history of the New **Testament**.

Until the 19th century, most Christians believed that the gospels were eye-witness accounts of the life of Jesus. Then it became clear that this could not be true as there were differences in the texts over some important pieces of information. For example, not all lists of the apostles are the same and the order of events is different between the four accounts. These differences do not really matter once it is accepted that these are the best attempts to record the details some 40 to 80 years after Jesus' death.

Luke 1:1–4

Many have undertaken to draw up an account of the things that have been fulfilled among us, just as they were handed down to us by those who from the first were eyewitnesses and servants of the word. Therefore, since I myself have carefully investigated everything from the beginning, it seemed good also to me to write an orderly account for you, most excellent Theophilus, so that you may know the certainty of the things you have been taught.

Characteristics	Matthew	Mark	Luke	John
Probably one of the 12 apostles	Yes	Probably	No	Probably not
The apostle who probably influenced the gospel writer	Matthew	Peter	Paul (although he was not one of the original 12 apostles)	The Beloved Disciple
Probable date of writing	Between 70 and 90 CE	Some scholars place this at 64 CE	Between 70 and 90 CE	Around 110 CE
Original language	Greek with some Aramaic expressions	Primitive Greek with some Aramaic expressions	Sophisticated Greek	Greek
Probable intended audience	The early Christian community in Jerusalem	The early Christian community in Rome	Christians in Mediterranean Churches founded by Paul	Christians in and around Asia Minor
Stories of Jesus' birth and childhood	Yes	No	Yes	No

Catholic uses of the gospels

Catholics see the gospels as the most important sacred texts of their Church. There is a reading from the gospel at every Mass, and it is usual for the priest to preach his sermon on its theme. The stand in a church from which sacred texts are read is known as a **lectern**. On Palm Sunday there are two gospel readings, one that retells the story of Jesus entering Jerusalem, and the other, much longer one, which relates Jesus' passion, suffering and death. At other times Catholics will pick important sections of the gospels to:

- support a point they are trying to make
- give evidence of what Jesus might have said or done about an issue
- create a themed liturgy for a special occasion
- settle a dispute over a matter of belief or morality.

FOR DEBATE

The gospels tell the highlights of Jesus' life, mission, death and resurrection. This is a good news story of the salvation of the world and of the human race. Salvation means 'saving' and is used to show how Jesus saved the world from the slavery of sin. Ask yourself and your work partners, 'Is the salvation of the world really good news?'

Jesus' teaching in the gospels

Catholics looking for guidance will often turn to the passages of the gospels known as the 'Sermon on the Mount' or, in Luke's case 'the Sermon on the Plain'. Here the gospel writers have compiled many of Jesus' sayings on prayer, human behaviour, how to get into Heaven, what to do if persecuted – that is, a whole range of things.

These sermons would have been very useful for the early Church as it tried to work out how it was different from its Jewish origins. They serve as a reminder to Catholics today that following Jesus can be difficult, challenging and occasionally dangerous. They are also important manifestos of faith, equality, justice, and charity.

AO1 skills ACTIVITIES

Some Catholics believe the gospels are all that is needed for salvation. Choose one gospel passage and analyse how it shows Catholics the path to God.

New Testament writings

The next two pages will help you to:

- examine the types of literature in the New Testament
- identify the reasons for the inclusion of particular books in the New Testament
- evaluate the use of New Testament literature to support beliefs and values.

The Four Horsemen of the Apocalypse (Albrecht Dürer) Revelation 6:1–8.

AO1 skills ACTIVITIES

For many people, modern forms of communication have replaced the custom of letter writing. Choose a paragraph from St Paul and write it as a text message. Describe how and explain why the letters of St Paul have stood the test of time in their original form.

Communicating a story

Suppose you wanted to tell lots of people about an amazing experience you had one weekend. Today you might send a text message to your friends or you might create a blog or web page. Two thousand years ago such technologies were not available and most stories passed around by word of mouth. This is called the 'oral tradition'. One of the problems with this is that it only takes one person to get the message wrong and the story gets changed when it is retold.

In the time of Jesus, really important events were recorded by officials or civil servants. That is how we know so much about the ancient Romans, Greeks and Jews. We have their records and many of their important documents.

St Paul was both a Roman citizen and a Jewish leader. He was learned and literate – unlike most people – so he could write down what he saw, the things he believed and his ideas for the future of the Church. He did this in the form of letters, which he sent to the leaders of Christian communities he founded as he travelled across the Middle East and southern Europe spreading the good news of Jesus' salvation.

Philippians 1:1–2

Paul and Timothy, servants of Christ Jesus,
To all the saints in Christ Jesus at Philippi, together with the overseers and deacons:
Grace and peace to you from God our Father and the Lord Jesus Christ.

Luke's record of the Acts of the Apostles

One of Paul's comrades in his travels was the man who has become known as Luke the **Evangelist**, or **gospel** writer. It seems as though he wrote down the stories of Jesus as retold by Paul. These must have come from one of the other apostles, because Paul was an enemy of Jesus before he was crucified. However, his book of the Acts of the Apostles is more like an eye-witness account or chronicle, since he features as one of the characters within it. This book is more like the historical books of the Old **Testament** that tell the stories of the kings and rulers of Israel.

Revelations

The **Bible** closes with the Book of Revelation. The writing in this book is colourful and is packed with symbols and ideas. It is an attempt to describe what the end of time will be like and how Christians will be able to take their place in Heaven. It is prophetic and visionary and is a powerful insight into the hopes and fears of the early Christian community. Scholars are unsure of its original authorship but have shown how it draws on some parts of the Old Testament for its inspiration.

REMEMBER THIS

Paul would have written his letters in Greek, since this was the most common language at the time. He would have used a form that would have been free from dialect or local idioms. For that reason his letters are very clear. This explains the influence these writings have had on the development of Catholic thought. Other writers' ideas may well have got 'lost in **translation**'.

AO2 skills ACTIVITIES

Examine the benefits of reading all the books in the New Testament. Write a script between two Catholics: one who supports this idea and another who thinks only the gospels should be read. Role-play the parts.

The New Testament informs Catholic practice, worship, beliefs and behaviour. Create an advert that would encourage young Catholics to read it today.

Catholic versions of the Bible

The next two pages will help you to:

- identify and name Catholic versions of the Bible
- explain the reasons why Catholics have different versions of the Bible
- consider the value of different versions.

The Bible and the vernacular

One of the principal outcomes of the Reformation (see Topic 3.4) was the emergence of editions of the **Bible** in the **vernacular**. Part of the reason for this was the liberating effect of people being able to read the stories of Jesus in their own language. Until that time they had only been able to read the Bible in Latin. This meant that interpretations of the content and meaning of the **scriptures** were controlled by the clergy.

The existence of schools is a legacy of the need to train clergymen to learn, interpret and preach the scriptures. Literacy strategies, in the Middle Ages, were aimed at enabling priests to read.

Latin had been the formal language of the Roman Empire and by the time of the Reformation it was the official language of the Holy Roman Empire, the head of which was the Pope.

This copy of the Bible in the Vulgate edition was printed in 1618 CE.

The Vulgate

Another reason why Martin Luther and other reformers were keen to have the Bible in their own language was their belief that the Church was reading from an inaccurate version of the scriptures. At the time, the Bible in use was known as the Vulgate. The name comes from the same word as 'vulgar' in Latin and suggests that it was a Bible aimed at the common people.

This version had been **translated** from the ancient Hebrew and Greek but also from a fully Greek version called the *Septuagint*. This had allegedly been assembled by 70 (or 72) scholars working on the ancient texts, who completed the task in 72 days – a remarkable achievement in the days when copying would have been done by hand.

AO1 skills ACTIVITIES

Identify the additional writings included in the Catholic Bible and explain where they came from. Describe one story or event contained within these writings. Give reasons for your choice.

The Apocrypha

Included in later versions of the Vulgate were the books now known as the **Apocrypha** which, although part of the Jewish heritage, had been written in Greek, not Hebrew. The reformers believed that it was not appropriate to have Old **Testament** texts which Jesus would probably not have read in the Bible. Protestant versions of the Bible, therefore, excluded them. The six books of the Apocrypha are: Tobias, Judith, Wisdom of Solomon, Baruch/Ecclesiasticus, First book of Maccabees and Second book of Maccabees.

The first English Bible

The influence of the Reformation on Europe was extensive. One of the ways in which the Catholic Church was affected was in the realisation that it needed to have its own accurate vernacular version(s) of the Bible so that it could counter the arguments of the reformers. The translation work to produce an English version of the Bible was undertaken by Gregory Martin at the English College in Douay, near Flanders in Belgium, and in Oxford. Most modern English Catholic Bibles are based on this later translation.

The Jerusalem Bible

In the 1970s, after the Second Vatican Council, when the Church was trying to modernise itself, a new version of the Bible was published. It is known as the Jerusalem Bible and is used in churches and schools across the UK and in other English-speaking Catholic Communities. In 1985 this was updated by the New Jerusalem Bible which is the version used in this book and the one that the readings for the mass are taken from.

The teachings of the early Church fathers

It is important to note that as well as scriptures contained within the Bible, Catholics also pay great respect to the teachings and writings of the early Church fathers. This explains a major difference between Catholics and Protestants. Martin Luther sought justification for his beliefs in 'scripture alone' whereas Catholics have always argued for truth found in 'scripture and tradition'.

MUST THINK ABOUT!

Some of the Apocrypha refer to events in the history of Israel that occurred about 300 years before Jesus' birth. This period is known as the restoration and was a time when the Jews asserted their independence from Seleucid empire. Their leader was a man called Judas Maccabeus who, having defeated the enemies of the Jews, cleansed the Temple and relit the lamps to show that God was there.

AO2 skills ACTIVITIES

The passing on of the faith is very important to Catholics. Prepare arguments for a class discussion on how important scripture is in this process of teaching young Catholics about their faith.

Vatican documents

The next two pages will help you to:

- examine the texts Catholics use to support their belief system
- explain the relationship between these texts and the texts of the Bible
- evaluate the claims to authority implied in these texts.

Pope Benedict XVI signing the 2007 encyclical Spes Salvi (In hope we are saved).

AO1 skills ACTIVITIES

Describe and explain the purpose of Vatican documents. Using the Internet, either in class or later, make a list of the Vatican documents written by Pope Benedict XVI.

Authority in the Church

Catholics believe that Jesus handed authority for the leadership of the Church to St Peter. Authority, they believe, flows through all those successors of the first Bishop of Rome who are known as the Pope (apostolic succession). If a Pope says something, people across the world listen. If the Pope writes something down, it acquires special significance. It is for this reason that documents that come from the Vatican are regarded as holy.

Vatican documents

Vatican documents are always published first in Latin and are only then **translated** into the **vernacular** so that there can be no doubt about what they say. There have been some very famous documents containing very important messages. The document *Populorum Progressio* (1967), on the development of peoples, was a clear statement by the Church of its commitment to the poor and its approach to 20th century politics. *Humanae Vitae* (1968), on human life, became famous for its critical stance on contraception and artificial methods of birth control.

Papal encyclicals

The most common way for a Pope to get his message to the people is by sending an encyclical. This is like a round-robin letter that some people send at Christmas to all their friends and family, to update them on all their news. The word 'encyclical' comes from the Greek word '*encyclios*', which means 'general'.

Bishops also send pastoral letters to each parish in their diocese to set out important pieces of information or new items of knowledge.

Before issuing an encyclical through a process called promulgation, the Pope will consult his advisors in the Vatican. These are usually high-ranking officials – rather like civil servants – who help shape each document so that it says exactly what the Pope intends it to say. He may also ask for experts in the specific area to provide wisdom on the issue. To help with this, the Vatican has its own colleges and places of study, as well as its own observatory.

'Gaudium et Spes', 1965

The joys and hopes, the griefs and the anxieties of the men of this age, especially those who are poor or in any way afflicted, these are the joys and hopes, the griefs and anxieties of the followers of Christ. Indeed, nothing genuinely human fails to raise an echo in their hearts. For theirs is a community composed of men.

Look at the quotation from '*Gaudium et Spes*'. This document is also known as 'The Church in the Modern World' and was a powerful expression of how the Church saw itself during the Second Vatican Council. This was an era of great social and moral change and a time when the old order within the world was beginning to slip away, giving new, fresh and exciting ideas the chance to flourish. The Fathers of the Church saw this and realised that change was necessary.

MUST THINK ABOUT!

The Church continues to teach about contemporary moral issues, even though Jesus did not leave any specific sayings on them. For example, nuclear weapons, contraception, global warming or IVF could not have been issues in his lifetime, but the Church takes its lead on these issues from the principles Jesus did lay out. The Church continues to make new doctrine (teaching) on its own evaluation of the world as it is now. A Catholic may think about moral issues in the light of what Jesus may have said.

AO1 skills ACTIVITIES

Imagine you had the authority to write a Vatican document. This would be read by Catholics all around the world. What would you write it on and why?

Topic 6.7

The Bible in worship

The next two pages will help you to:

- identify the occasions when the Bible might be used in worship
- illustrate how a priest might use the Bible to support his preaching.

For Christians, the Bible is the revealed word of God.

The Bible as an aid to prayer and reflection

The **Bible** is a gateway to understanding how people in the Old **Testament**, and at the time of Jesus, thought about the world. Today it provides Catholics with similar insights into how they should react to or respond to the situations that they meet in life. One of the main roles of the priesthood is to explain how the **scriptures** can help.

In Topics 6.3 and 6.4, you read about the various sections of the Bible that are used in Mass. It is normal for the readings to follow this pattern:

- Old Testament
- Psalm
- New Testament
- the **Gospel** Acclamation (usually a verse from one of the Psalms)
- Gospel.

AO1 skills **ACTIVITIES**

The Bible is full of good and interesting advice. Choose five pieces of biblical advice and explain their relevance in the lives of people today.

The sermon

After the readings, it is normal for the priest to preach a sermon or homily about their content. Since they normally follow a theme, or are directly related to the liturgical calendar in some way, it is quite easy for the priest to find support or guidance for what he wants to say. In the sermon, the priest will give spiritual leadership and guidance to the community. Priests are trained for this activity and they will supplement the knowledge and understanding acquired while training with new knowledge gathered from continuous reading or study.

In recent times, lay people and deacons have been encouraged to take on the role of preaching, and many lead Bible study groups with groups of parishioners or other members of the Church. There are many more opportunities for lay people to learn about and study the scriptures than there used to be. Interpreting biblical texts for the modern world is a task that can be undertaken by anybody willing to study them hard and to make connections to the world today.

The Bible as a source of wisdom and guidance

Jesus said some interesting things, which have to be interpreted to understand their meaning. For example: 'it is easier for a camel to pass through the eye of a needle than for someone rich to enter the kingdom of heaven' (Matthew 19:24b).

Of course, it would be impossible for a camel to actually pass through the eye of a needle. It is possible that Jesus was referring to a gate in the city wall of Jerusalem through which a camel could pass, providing its owner had removed the bags and panniers that would have been strapped to it to transport goods and products. This is a metaphor. Jesus was saying that rich people needed to free themselves of all their attachment to earthly goods if they wanted to enter a rich new life with God.

We know also that Jesus included wealthy people in his company, like Joseph of Arimathaea. We know this because only a rich person could have afforded the kind of tomb that was prepared for Jesus' body after his crucifixion. Joseph clearly decided that one of the ways he could best show his love for God was by providing love, support and comfort to Jesus' immediate family after his death. This is a powerful model for those coming after him. Catholics read the stories in the Bible and interpret them as best they can for meaning and relevance in their daily lives.

FOR DEBATE

Discuss this statement with your class: 'There should be no such thing as a boring sermon; it is the priest's job to make the word of God as interesting as possible.'

AO2 skills ACTIVITIES

Imagine you are the prosecutor in a court of law. Outline the case you would make to the judge to show how the Bible is valued above all other books in both private and public worship. Be prepared to share your evidence with the class.

'The Bible is too difficult for people to understand today.' Write a reasoned response to such a view, remembering to conclude with your own informed opinion.

Approaches to scripture

The next two pages will help you to:

- identify what people mean when they say that the Bible is true
- account for the differences in approaches
- present your own opinion about the truth of the scriptures.

'The betrayal of Christ' by Fra Angelico.

Conservative approaches to scripture

Some people believe that the **Bible** is literally the word of God, that God dictated his ideas and that a human wrote them down before turning them into actual books. This conservative approach to **scripture** is called 'fundamentalism'. Fundamentalists often also adopt a creationist approach to the origins of the world, believing that God created the world in six days and rested on the seventh. They believe this because they approach the Bible as if it were literally true. The problem with this approach is that it can make God look rather inconsistent and contradictory.

AO1 skills ACTIVITIES

Christians believe the Bible is 'the word of God in human words'. Explain what this means and how it sometimes results in denominations interpreting the events and stories in different ways.

Orthodox approaches to scripture

Catholics who believe that the Bible is the word of God in the words of men are described as being 'orthodox' in their approach. This means that they see the Bible as inspired by God and that the ideas, concepts and stories were the products of the writers' reflections on earlier wisdom, the experiences they had had and their belief system. They turned these into stories which showed that God was 'on their side'. The problem with this approach is that other people, with different interpretations, think God is on their side too.

MUST THINK ABOUT!

If Jesus needed to die in order to enable Catholics to go to Heaven and Judas caused Jesus to die by his betrayal, is it the case that Judas had God on his side?

Liberal approaches to scripture

Most Catholic Bible scholars have a liberal view of the Bible: they see it as a collection of ancient texts that emerged from the remnants of the Roman Empire and were put together by Fathers of the Church, such as St Irenaeus of Lyons and St Jerome. They believe that the Bible has always been open to interpretation and that much of the Bible is commentary on the events of the time that first the Jews and then early Christians were experiencing.

It is recognised that the Bible contains myths, legends, pieces of preaching and teaching and quite a lot of opinion. They believe that it can be a guide for living in the 21st century but that judgments on which it is based are also open to interpretation. The problem with this approach is that it is possible to justify almost anything using the Bible.

Scripture as parable

Biblical scholars have shown that much of what the Bible has to say is presented in symbolic language. Jesus used parables extensively in his teaching. The word 'parable' can be used to describe the words of God in the words of humans. Adopting this approach enables readers to see, for example, the creation story as a parable, the feeding of the thousands as a metaphor for Jesus' ability to influence a number of people, or the Book of Revelation as a way for Christians to explain the end of time.

Mark 8:1–10

And now once again a great crowd had gathered, and they had nothing to eat. So he called his disciples to him and said to them, 'I feel sorry for all these people; they have been with me for three days now and have nothing to eat. If I send them off home hungry they will collapse on the way; some have come a great distance.'

His disciples replied, 'Where could anyone get these people enough bread to eat in a deserted place?' He asked them, 'How many loaves have you?' And they said to him, 'Seven.' Then he instructed the crowd to sit down on the ground, and he took the seven loaves, and after giving thanks he broke them and began handing them to his disciples to distribute; and they distributed them among the crowd.

They had a few small fishes as well, and over these he said a blessing and ordered them to be distributed too. They ate as much as they wanted, and they collected seven basketfuls of the scraps left over. Now there had been about four thousand people. He sent them away and at once, getting into the boat with his disciples, went to the region of Dalmanutha.

AO2 skills ACTIVITIES

Pope Benedict XVI once wrote that 'the study of the Bible is never finished'. Assess the impact of this statement for Catholics today in their understanding of scripture and their attitudes to other Christians.

Examine how far the Bible should be taken literally. Give examples to support the strengths and weaknesses of this approach.

Topic 6.9

The authority of the Bible in the 21st century

The next two pages will help you to:

- explore passages in the Bible that some see as controversial
- explain the reasons why Catholics still rely on scripture
- come to an informed judgement on the authority of the Bible.

The Hereford Mappa Mundi (map of the world c.1300).

AO1 skills ACTIVITIES

Write a paragraph setting out your point of view on how the world was created. Compare this with the accounts of the creation in Genesis chapters 1 and 2. Of the two biblical accounts, which do you think is more likely to be true? Record your response to this question.

The Bible and the Universe

Some people see the world in white and black; others see it in shades of grey. The boundaries between things get more blurred as more becomes known about the world and the way it is. Some things that were once regarded as true have now been proved to be false. For example, until the 15th century many people believed that the universe revolved around the earth. Much of this thinking came from the biblical account of creation.

In the **Bible**, if people wanted to get nearer to God they went up mountains – think of Moses on Mount Sinai and Jesus on Mount Tabor. The clouds on the top of mountains were thought of as the glory of God in the Hebrew mind. Water, on the other hand, was used to describe chaos and devastation – think of the Flood or Moses passing through the Red Sea.

The Bible as a guide to living

Catholics accept the findings of modern science. They will also use the Bible as a guide for living. They tend to balance Biblical teaching against their own gut reaction to what they believe to be true and their reasoned approaches to issues – this is often referred to as conscience.

The Bible and behaviour

There are some human behaviours that the Bible reports accurately. People tend to spread their beliefs around rather than concentrating on one complete system. They tend to be selfish, using time to pursue their own interests and activities. Respect for parents, elders and authority figures is often overlooked, and people lie, steal and form inappropriate sexual relationships. Murder is committed regularly, which leads to unhappiness, anger and, often, retaliatory killings.

Various stories in the Bible highlight these things and warn readers about doing the same. In this sense it can be seen as a source of moral wisdom, even if some of its stories are not word for word true.

The Bible and women

There are several instances where the Bible provides teaching which can be challenging. The following quotations are seen by some as controversial:

- 'Wive should be subject to their husband as to the Lord.' (Ephesians 5:22).
- 'Women are to remain quiet in the assemblies, since they have no permission to speak: theirs is a subordinate part, as the law itself says.' (1 Corinthians 14:34).
- 'Son of man, the members of the House of Israel used to live in their own territory, but they defiled it by their conduct and actions; to me their conduct was as unclean as a woman's menstruation.' (Ezekiel 36:17).

What do you think of this? Is your response likely to be affected by your own gender?

MUST THINK ABOUT!

In the Old **Testament**, Abraham was commanded by God to take his son Isaac to the top of a mountain, build an altar and sacrifice him. Suppose God asked you to sacrifice your firstborn child what would you do, especially if you had waited about 80 years for the gift of a child?

AO2 skills ACTIVITIES

The Magisterium is the official teaching office of the Catholic Church. It states the rules that Catholics should follow in matters of faith (belief) and practice (behaviour). Assess the benefits and disadvantages for Catholics of such clear direction.

The importance of the Bible in the 21st century

The next two pages will help you to:

- explain why Catholics regard the Bible as important in the 21st century
- explain the contribution the Bible makes to Catholic moral teaching
- prepare a moral argument using the Bible as a source of inspiration or justification.

Catholics should always try to help the homeless.

The Bible as a guide

You should now understand the orthodox Catholic approach to the **Bible**. The Bible is seen as a collection of powerful stories which present symbolic approaches to the issues of the day and the challenges facing modern Catholics. Guidance is given through the words and works of people whose stories are recorded in the Biblical texts. Above all, the teachings and actions of Jesus become models for Catholics to use as a means of informing their conscience.

Jesus as the guide

Some Christians will constantly ask 'What would Jesus do? – often abbreviated as WWJD? It is impossible to know what Jesus would have done when confronted with 21st-century problems. His reactions and responses to the issues of his time can be taken as a form of moral compass. The table shows some examples of his guidance.

AO1 skills ACTIVITIES

Read the parable of the Sheep and the Goats in Matthew 25:31–46. This parable is widely accepted as the basis for Christian living. Place Jesus' instructions into a chart with appropriate labels and drawings.

FOR DEBATE

Jesus taught that his followers should visit prisoners. Organise a discussion in your class considering whether there are any categories of prisoners that you would not wish to visit. Create a presentation to the rest of the class giving reasons for your selection.

MUST THINK ABOUT!

It is often said that it is not good to mix religion and politics. Jesus was executed for treason because of his constant criticism of the Jewish and Roman authorities. Should Catholics be critical of political systems and the way in which they operate?

Issue	Example from the Bible
Non-violent ways of solving disputes	You have heard how it was said: 'Eye for eye and tooth for tooth.' But I say this to you: 'Offer no resistance to the wicked. On the contrary, if anyone hits you on the right cheek, offer him the other as well'. (Matthew 5:38–39) You have heard how it was said, 'You will love your neighbour and hate your enemy.' But I say this to you, 'Love your enemies and pray for those who persecute you', so that you may be children of your Father in heaven. (Matthew 5:43–45a)
Caring for the poor	Jesus looked steadily at him and he was filled with love for him, and he said, 'You need to do one thing more. Go and sell what you own and give the money to the poor, and you will have treasure in heaven; then come, follow me'. (Mark 10:21) You have the poor with you always, and you can be kind to them whenever you wish, but you will not always have me. (Mark 14:7) Then fixing his eyes on his disciples he said: 'How blessed are you who are poor: the kingdom of God is yours'. (Luke 6:20)
Treatment of neighbours	I give you a new commandment: 'Love one another; you must love one another just as I have loved you'. It is by your love for one another, that everyone will recognise you as my disciples. (John 13:34–35) He replied, 'You must love the Lord your God with all your heart, with all your soul, with all your strength, and with all your mind, and your neighbour as yourself.' (Luke 10:27)
Treatment of sinners	They asked him this as a test, looking for an accusation to use against him. But Jesus bent down and started writing on the ground with his finger. As they persisted with their question, he straightened up and said, 'Let the one among you who is guiltless be the first to throw a stone at her.' (John 8:6–7)

Much of what Jesus said and did went against the customs and practices of the Jewish people or the Romans who controlled them. He can be said to have acted against the culture of the time because he saw much of it as wrong and offensive to God's plan for the world. Catholics believe that they, too, should stand out against things that are wrong.

Using the Bible to support a reasoned argument

This last section has an underlying theme which comes from Latin American Catholics. They believe that Jesus made an 'Option for the Poor' and use many of the quotations above to support their arguments. In Religious Studies, it is important to back up any argument with evidence or reasons. The Bible can be used in this way. Some Catholics will even engage with the practice of allowing a Bible to fall open, closing their eyes and putting a pin on the page to see if the place it lands points to any particular wisdom or guidance. It is surprising the number of people who allow their lives to be directed by this kind of Biblical lottery.

AO2 skills ACTIVITIES

Respond to the comment that all the Catholic teaching on social justice is contained within the parable of the Sheep and the Goats.

Catholics often compare life to a journey. A journey without a map or a guide could be dangerous. After considering the pressures and problems of 21st-century living, assess, with examples, how the Bible might prove a worthy guide for Catholics today.

GradeStudio

Welcome to the Grade Studio

GCSE is about what you can do, not what you can't do. You need to know what examiners want in your answers so that you can get the best possible marks. In GCSE Religious Studies there are two things that examiners are looking for. These are called assessment objectives (AO). Questions are designed to help examiners find out how well you do in each assessment objective.

Graded examples for this topic

AO1

AO1 questions test what you know and how well you can explain and analyse things. Let's look at an AO1 question to see what examiners are expecting you to do.

Question

State one part of the Bible. **[1 mark]**

Possible steps to answer the question: What should an answer be like and how do examiners work out what is a good or a poor response?

This is an AO1 question, meaning it is trying to test your knowledge and understanding.

Get used to thinking of the word 'state' as the flag for a factual response. There are three possible answers: the Old Testament, the New Testament and the apocrypha.

Question

State two kinds of literature found in the Bible.

[2 marks]

Choose two kinds of literature you could write about in more detail if you needed to, in a later part of the question. The 6-mark AO1 question or the 12-mark AO2 question could depend on what you choose in this part. Two good examples to use would be poetry and history.

Question

Give three reasons why Catholics say the Bible is important. **[3 marks]**

Notice the use of 'give' instead of 'state'. It is just another flag word for a factual response. Possible reasons include:

1 The Bible teaches about people who have been close to God, such as the Prophets.
2 The Bible tells the story of the life of Jesus.
3 The Bible is the word of God.

Question

Explain why the gospels are important to Christians.

[6 marks]

There are three levels for AO1, but this does not mean that there are two marks per level. Examiners are looking for depth of understanding, which might be shown by referring to several different reasons briefly or by considering two reasons fully. You could build a good response in this way.

Level 1	Begin with the most obvious point: Catholics believe that the gospels contain information about Jesus and so are significant for Christians because he is the founder of the faith.
Level 2	Develop this either by referring to another reason, such as the belief that the gospels were written by people who had first-hand experience of Jesus and are therefore reliable, or by expanding the first point by describing the kind of information about Jesus that they contain and explaining why this is important. For example, they show Jesus to be the saviour by his actions and by his death and resurrection.
Level 3	Expand this with reference to other important contents of the gospels, such as Jesus' moral teaching in the 'Sermon on the Mount'. Then draw the aspects of the response together with a comment about how, because of these contents, the gospels are crucial in keeping Christians in touch with what the first Christians believed.

AO2

Question

Some parts of the Bible are so out of date they should be removed. **[12 marks]**

Remember that for AO2 questions, responses must give different views about the issue in the question, and for Level 4, you must give your own view. Views must be supported with evidence and argument. Examiners use levels of response that enable them to credit a wide range of responses, but to ensure that you reach the highest level you need to build the response through the levels in an organised way. Let's now look at what you need to do to achieve a high level.

Level 1 The candidate will demonstrate little understanding of the question. The answer will be too simple with little or no relevant information.	Explain the significance of the issue in the statement and then offer at least one view about it. Identify a part of the Bible that could be considered out of date and use it as an example for discussion. You could select a story from the Old Testament that suggests that God is a violent God, such as the plagues experienced by the Egyptians or the slaughter of Israel's enemies by Joshua or King David. Or you could choose the story of creation in Genesis, which seems to contradict modern scientific knowledge.
Level 2 The candidate will show some understanding of the question. Some relevant information will be included but often the answer is one-sided.	Go on to develop the response by explaining the way in which the material chosen is out of date, perhaps because science has better explanations for the beginning of the world.
Level 3 The candidate will show a satisfactory understanding of the question with a range of relevant material and appropriate evidence.	Offer an alternative view, with justification. For example, the Bible records how people gradually began to understand that God was a loving God. The bloody history and particular understanding of the nature of God gradually gives way, through the Old Testament prophets, to the God of love in the teaching of Jesus. Give your own view.
Level 4 The candidate will show a clear understanding of the question with a range of fully supported viewpoints backed by relevant evidence and argument.	Now support your own view and support it with evidence and argument. For example, you could say that it would be wrong to remove parts of the Bible because it is all part of the rich tradition of the Church, but this does not mean all parts should be given equal status. So for Christians the New Testament is more important but they need the Old Testament as well to understand the novelty of Jesus' life and teaching. Or you could say that much of it is out of date and could be ignored.

These specimen answers provide an outline of how you could construct your response. Space does not allow us to give a full response. The examiner will be looking for more detail in your actual exam responses.

Remember and Reflect

AO1 Describe, explain and analyse, using knowledge and understanding

Question	Find the answer on:
1 Identify four types of literature in the Bible.	PAGE 152–153
2 Why is the Old Testament sometimes referred to as the Hebrew scriptures?	PAGE 147
3 What does the word 'gospel' mean?	PAGE 150
4 Name two New Testament authors other than the four main gospel writers.	PAGE 153
5 Explain the differences in approach to the scriptures of: *a fundamentalist Catholics* *b orthodox Catholics* *c liberal Catholics*	PAGE 159–160
6 Why do most non-Catholics have 39 books in the Old Testament whereas Catholics have 45?	PAGE 155
7 Who was the first Englishman to translate the Bible from the Latin?	PAGE 155
8 What was Martin Luther's contribution to the development of the Bible?	PAGE 154
9 What is an evangelist?	PAGE 145
10 According to the gospels, where did Jesus go when he wanted to read from the scriptures?	PAGE 147
11 Identify two reasons why Catholics still refer to the Bible.	PAGE 164–166
12 What is the function of a lectern in church?	PAGE 145
13 How long does it take to read through the whole Bible in sequence?	PAGE 148
14 What is meant by the 'oral tradition'?	PAGE 152
15 Where in the Bible will you find the book of Revelation and what is it about?	PAGE 153
16 Name at least two important Vatican documents.	PAGE 157
17 Explain the function of a papal encyclical.	PAGE 157
18 Which parts of the scriptures are used at Mass?	PAGE 151
19 Give four examples of Jesus' moral teaching that are still relevant today.	PAGE 165

AO2 Use evidence and reasoned argument to express and evaluate personal responses, informed insights, and differing viewpoints

1 'If it says in the Bible that God made the world in six days, it must be true.' How do you respond to this statement? What is your view?

2 Some of the characteristics of God that are displayed in the Old Testament make him appear to be angry, jealous, destructive and frightening. Lots of people report being afraid in his presence. What do you think of this? Does this coincide with your image of God?

3 'If Jesus had lived now he would have used the Internet to get his message across.' Do you agree with this statement? Give reasons for your answer.

4 Why do you think there are contradictions and differences between the gospel accounts of stories from the life of Jesus? Explain the thinking behind your response, with reference to at least two stories from the gospels.

5 Do you think readings from other sources should be included in Sunday worship, for example poems on spiritual themes or extracts from the books of holy men and women?

6 Catholics believe that the Pope is the representative of Jesus on Earth. Should more of the writings or teachings of the Pope be read out as part of the liturgy? Support your argument – for or against – with evidence and good reasons.

7 Have you ever played 'Biblical roulette'? This is the practice of allowing a Bible to fall open and then sticking a pin somewhere on the page and reading the verse to which it points to see if it has anything relevant to say in your life. Do you think this is a good idea or not?

8 Which of these people, in your opinion, made the biggest contribution to the Bible as it is today: St Irenaeus of Lyons, Martin Luther or Gregory Martin? Give reasons for your answer.

Welcome

Welcome to Exam Café. Here you can get ready for your exam through a range of revision tools and exam preparation activities designed to help you get the most out of your revision time.

Tools and Tips

Now you have finished the course/Topic, it is time to revise and prepare for the examination. A key to any exam is the revision and preparation leading up to it. The key to good revision is to 'work smart'. This section will guide you in knowing what is needed for success and, just as important, what is not. So don't panic! Think positive because the examiner will. GCSE is about what you *can* do, not what you can't.

Key points to note at this stage

1 Your revision will need to focus on what the examiner is looking for in the answers so that you can achieve the best possible mark. Remember that the examiners are looking for the AO1 and AO2 assessment objectives. Each of these objectives is worth 50 per cent of the total mark.

2 You also need to know that the exam questions on the paper are designed to test your performance with both AO1 and AO2 objectives. Each question will be made up of five parts:

- Four AO1 parts, of which three check your knowledge and one tests your understanding and analysis
- One question testing AO2 – your ability to consider different points of view on a particular issue and how much you can express your own points of view with relevant evidence and argument.

Once you understand what the examiner is looking for, it will be time to turn to your revision programme.

How to get started

An important key to success with any exam is the preparation beforehand. While few people enjoy the process of revision, it is something that is vital for success. Your class teacher will also discuss revision with you. Below are some suggestions and ideas that can be employed:

1 It is vital to revise in plenty of time before the exam. Do not leave everything to the last minute.

2 Design a revision timetable and be realistic about what can be achieved.

3 Revision is a personal matter and we all learn in different ways. Remember that many revision skills can be transferred between different subjects.

4 These are some suggested revision techniques:

- Create summary cards for each topic – a maximum of 5–10 bullet points on each card.
- Create lists of key words and terms. Ask somebody to test you on them or hang them around the house.
- Create a mind map to summarise a major topic.
- Design cards with a word or idea on one side and a question/definition or answer on the other. These allow you to be tested by family members or friends who may not have much subject knowledge.
- Create an A–Z list on a certain topic. This involves writing the 26 letters of the alphabet down the side of a page and then having to write a key word or teaching connected to that topic for each letter.
- Remember that religious teachings do not have to be learned word-for-word. It is acceptable to paraphrase them.

5 Break your revision sessions of 5–10 minutes to start with (this can be increased as you become much better at it). Give yourself a short break (of about 5 minutes) and then go back to revising. Remember that spending time revising when nothing is going in is as bad as doing no revision at all.

6 Try answering questions on past papers then marking them with the mark scheme yourself. Alternatively, you can write your own questions and develop your own mark scheme. Answer the questions and use the levels of response to mark them.

7 Finally, remember that if you go into revision with a negative attitude you are ultimately going to make it much tougher on yourself.

Revision

Common errors and mistakes

So the day of the exam has arrived. Remember that you are not the first to sit exams and you will not be the last. However, learn from the experience of others and do not fall into any of the following exam traps:

Misreading the question: Take a minute and read the question carefully. Surprisingly, a large number of candidates do not read the questions properly. They simply see a word and feel they have to start writing. No matter how good your answer is, if it does not answer the question it will not gain you any marks.

Wasting valuable time: The exam is a race against the clock. Match the length of your response to the number of marks being awarded. A one-mark question can be answered with a single word or a sentence and not a paragraph.

Poor selection of knowledge: Choose good examples that help you to develop and explain your ideas.

Disorganised waffle: Written answers, especially AO2 style answers, require you to plan your answer carefully. It requires a range of viewpoints including religious responses and your own views. Be careful and do not let your own views take over.

Know the exam paper: Make sure that you fully understand the layout and instructions for the exam paper. In particular, focus on which questions you must do and how many questions you are required to do.

It is Religious Studies after all: Remember that the subject is Religious Studies and you will be tested on your knowledge and understanding of religion and its impact on the lives of individuals and communities. Make sure your answers contain relevant religious ideas.

Revision check list

The details of the course are known as the Specification. It is broken down into the Topics listed below. There is a summary of the key areas within each Topic that you need to know about.

TOPIC 1 CORE BELIEFS

For this Topic you must:

- know and understand the core beliefs of the Catholic Church
- know and understand the Nicene Creed, which is the fullest statement of the beliefs of the Catholic Church
- be able to explain the effects of these beliefs on the customs and practices of Catholics
- understand the impact of your developing knowledge and understanding on your own belief system.

TOPIC 2 SPECIAL DAYS AND PILGRIMAGES

For this Topic you must:

- know and understand the main festivals of the Catholic Church
- know and understand the important feast days of the Catholic Church
- know and understand some of the places of pilgrimage visited by Catholics
- be able to explain the reasons why Catholics celebrate or make pilgrimages.

TOPIC 3 MAJOR DIVISIONS AND INTERPRETATIONS

For this Topic you must:

- know and understand a short history of Christianity
- know and understand the major divisions between Catholicism and other Christian traditions
- be able to explain some of the different expressions of Catholicism around the world
- be able to explain those things that are shared by all Christians across the world.

TOPIC 4 PLACES AND FORMS OF WORSHIP

For this Topic you must:

- know and understand about cathedrals, churches and shrines
- know and understand the ways in which Catholics practise their faith in public
- be able to explain personal rituals and customs practised at home or in private.

TOPIC 5 RELIGION IN THE FAITH COMMUNITY AND THE FAMILY

For this Topic you must:

- know and understand the important rites and ceremonies that Catholics use to mark the stages of a person's life
- understand the meaning of 'community' and what it means to live in a community
- be able to explain the distinctive features of a Catholic community.

TOPIC 6 SACRED WRITINGS

For this Topic you must:

- know and understand the texts that Catholics consider to be sacred scriptures
- know and understand the place of the Bible in the canon of sacred literature
- know and understand other texts and writings that are considered holy by the Church
- be able to explain different approaches to the authority of the Bible
- be able to explain your own attitude to the authority of the Bible.

Exam preparation

Sample student answers

Now you have done some serious revision, it is time to see what sort of response to the questions will get good marks in the exam. Here are some examples of responses with comments from the examiner to show you what is good about them and how they could be improved.

Remember, examiners will use levels of response for part d, which is AO1 and part e, which is AO2. For parts a, b and c, responses will be point marked. This means that if there is one mark allocated for the question, only one point is expected, if two marks are allocated, then two points are expected and so on. Part a is worth one mark, b two marks and c three marks.

Here are some AO1 point-marked questions and example responses from Topic 1: Core beliefs.

What is a creed? **(1 mark)**

A creed is a statement of faith.

Examiner Tip

'What is?' just means describe something – in this case, a creed.

AO1 Part (d) questions

Some AO1 answers are marked in levels of response. These are part d of the questions and are worth six marks each. However, just because they are worth six marks, it does not mean that examiners want to see six short points or three developed points in the answer. Instead, the examiner is looking for a level of understanding. The higher the level then the higher the level of understanding required. This could be done by referring to several points and expanding each a little, or by developing one or two points in greater detail. Below is a sample answer.

Examiner Tip
When answering this question, ask yourself 'Why?' as soon as you have written down a reason. There are different levels of explanation, and the examiner is looking for depth, not for a superficial level.

Explain what Catholics believe about the Trinity. [6 marks]

Response 1

Catholics believe that the Trinity is how God is to be understood. The Trinity is God in three different forms: God the Father, God the Son and God the Holy Spirit. However, these are all one God.

Examiner says
This is satisfactory response, reaching Level 2. The information given is relevant, and accurate reasons have been chosen. However, the response is not well developed and needs more explanation.

Response 2

Catholics believe that the Holy Trinity is one way in which God can be understood. Catholics are monotheists and believe in one God. Therefore, the Trinity is this one God in three different forms or persons. These persons are God the Father, God the Son who is Jesus Christ and God the Holy Spirit, which continues to guide Christians in their lives today.

Catholics may pray just to God or to any of the persons of the Trinity. The Trinity is sometimes represented as a shamrock – one plant with three leaves joined together. However, these are all one God.

Examiner says
This is a good response. It contains much of the satisfactory response but it is much more developed. The reasons for different views are explained. This response would reach Level 3.

AO2

Part e of each question in the exam will involve an AO2 question asking you to explain different points of view about a particular issue. It also gives you an opportunity to present your own personal viewpoint. However, please remember that all viewpoints on a particular issue must be backed up with good evidence, argument and reasoning. Part e of each question is worth 12 marks, or 50 per cent of the total, so it is important to think carefully about how you are going to tackle these questions.

Planning an AO2 answer

These questions want different points of view about a particular issue. Your answer could therefore be structured in the following way:

Paragraph 1: Explain a view that will *agree* with the statement in the question. Offer evidence, beliefs and teachings to back up the point of view.

Paragraph 2: Explain a different view from what the statement is suggesting. Again, you need to offer evidence, beliefs and teachings to back up your point of view.

Paragraph 3: Include your own personal viewpoint about the issue raised. Again, you need to offer evidence, belief and arguments to support your point of view. The examiner does not mind which point of view you take, there is no right or wrong answer. Instead, the examiner is interested in your ability to reason and argue. If you really do not have a strong point of view on this issue just simply go for the viewpoint which you can best argue.

Here is an AO2 question and some example responses from Topic 2: Special days and pilgrimages.

'Christians should forget their differences and work together.' [12 marks]

Response 1

If all Christians are followers of Jesus then there is no reason why they should not all work and worship together.

Examiner says

This is Level 1. There is only one view and it has little support to back it up. This is a simplistic response and shows limited understanding of the question. There is no use of technical terms.

Response 2

If all Christians are followers of Jesus then there is no reason why they should not all work and worship together. In this way the Christian Church would be stronger and have more influence. Some Christians might feel that the differences between them are too important for them to be able to come together.

Examiner says

This is Level 2. This is a better answer as it explains to the examiner what the candidate understands the question to be about. However, although two viewpoints are stated and slightly developed, the response is still rather limited. Also, there is no personal view.

Response 3

If all Christians are followers of Jesus then there is no reason why they should not all work and worship together. In this way the Christian Church would be stronger and have more influence. Many Christians join ecumenical movements which try to bring Christians from different denominations together.

Some Christians might feel that the differences between them are too important for them to be able to come together. They may feel that they have different beliefs about, for example, the authority of the Pope or what happens at the eucharist and that these make it impossible for them to unite.

I think that if they really are all followers of Jesus then they should unite.

Examiner says

This is a satisfactory response and meets the criteria for Level 3. It is reasonably well organised and contains some significant views that are explained well and have evidence to justify them. There is a balance of views. There is good use of technical terms. However, the personal response is not supported and this limits the response to Level 3.

Response 4

If all Christians are followers of Jesus then there is no reason why they should not all work and worship together. In this way, the Christian Church would be stronger and have more influence. Many Christians join ecumenical movements which try to bring Christians from different denominations together.

Some Christians might feel that the differences between them are too important for them to be able to come together. They may feel that they have different beliefs about, for example, the authority of the Pope or what happens at the eucharist and that these make it impossible for them to unite.

I think that if they really are all followers of Jesus then everyone should work as hard as possible to unite into one Church for this must have been what Jesus and his followers intended.

Examiner says

The personal response presented is now supported and and comes to a conclusion. The candidate has grasped the significance of the issue. The personal view is backed up by evidence. There is good, accurate use of specialist terms and the response is reasonably well organised. This will take the response to Level 4.

Understanding exam language

Examiners try to keep questions short and clear. To do this they use special trigger words to hint at how you should respond to the questions. Below is a list of common trigger words. You should familiarise yourself with these words:

State Usually used in AO1 questions worth 1–3 marks. This means 'write down a fact about something'. For example, *State the name of the leader of Catholic worship in a church*.

Give This is used instead of 'state' and requires the same sort of response.

List This is used instead of 'give' or 'state' and requires the same sort of response.

Describe This is used in AO1 questions and means 'tell the examiner factual information about the item or idea'. An example is, *Describe events of Pentecost*, which means *write down factual information about the events of Pentecost*.

Give an account of This is asking for the same sort of response as 'describe'. For example, *Give an account of what happened at Pentecost*.

Explain This means 'show that you understand something'. For example, *Explain different Christian attitudes towards divorce*. An 'explain' response will include some knowledge, but the best responses will give a range of ideas and reasons.

Why This word is used as shorthand for 'explain'. Put the word 'explain' in front of it and you will know what to do. For example, *Why are there different Christian attitudes towards divorce?* is the same as *Explain why there are different Christian attitudes towards divorce*.

How This can be used to ask you for factual information. For example, *How do marriage ceremonies reflect Christian teaching?* It can also be used for questions that are asking for understanding where there is a mixture of fact and understanding required.

Important This word is used frequently in AO1 part d questions and it indicates that you say why someone should or should not do/ believe something. An example is, *Explain why the eucharist is important to Catholics*, which means, *Give reasons to explain why the eucharist is special to Catholics*.

Planning and structuring an answer

In the Grade Studios you have been shown how to build levels of response. This is really important for the AO1 responses to part d, worth six marks, and the AO2 responses to part e, worth 12 marks. In each case follow this structure:

- Check you really know what the question is asking. In the AO2 questions, work out the key word or words in the statement, for example, *Sacred books are too old to be useful today. Discuss this statement*. The key phrase here is *Discuss this statement*. If the answer does not deal with this then it will be awarded a low mark.
- Make a note of key points to include in all AO1 responses and use a diagram to note down viewpoints for AO2.
- Begin your answer with a brief mention of what the question is asking you to do.
- Write clearly and concisely. DON'T WAFFLE.
- Reach a conclusion at the end of your answer. In the case of an AO1 answer, this could be a brief summary sentence. For example, *So for these reasons Catholics might want to help the poor.* In the case of an AO2 answer, the conclusion should include a *personal view* (with supporting reasons/argument) and a *brief summing up* of the different views which you have expressed.
- Leave a gap of a few lines between each answer. This is in case you wish to add further ideas/information later (if you don't there is no need to worry).
- If you have any time left at the end of your exam, use it constructively. Check your answer makes sense. Check your answer is responding to the question set. Check your use of English, grammar and spelling. Check you have answered the required number of questions. *Remember, when you hand in your answer paper at the end of the exam, it is probably the last time you will ever see it. Make sure it is your best possible effort.*

absolution The pronouncement by a priest of the forgiveness of sins.

Advent The period beginning on the fourth Sunday before Christmas.

Anglican A member of the Church of England.

anointing of the sick Preparation for death by a priest anointing with holy oil and saying prayers.

Apocrypha Those books of the Bible that are included by Catholics but not other Christians.

apostle One of the twelve of Jesus' closest disciples. 'Apostle' means 'one who is sent' and is the name given to those who were sent out by Jesus to preach, to baptise and to gather the people into a Church.

Ash Wednesday The first day of Lent. In some Churches, penitents receive the sign of the Cross in ashes on their forehead.

baptism A ceremony where water is used as a symbol of washing away sin and starting life as a Christian.

believer's baptism Baptism of a young person or adult by total immersion in water as a sign that they have committed their life to Christ.

bereaved Feeling a deep sense of grief and loss at the death of a loved one.

Bible Christian holy book; from the Greek word *biblos* meaning 'book' or 'library'.

canon The agreed collection of books in the Bible.

Catholic A member of the Church of Rome (the word 'catholic' also means 'universal').

ceremony A formal procedure or service; specifically a religious ritual or service.

charity Giving to those in need.

Christ The anointed one. Messiah is used in the Jewish tradition to refer to the expected leader sent by God, who will bring salvation to God's people.

Christening Naming a baby.

Christian A believer in and follower of Jesus.

Christmas The festival commemorating the birth of Christ (25 December).

Church The word has three meanings, (i) the building where Christians worship, (ii) the congregation who worship in that building and who go out into the world to serve Jesus, and (iii) the fellowship of all believers.

confession Contrition; penance. (i) One of seven sacraments observed by some Churches whose priest confidentially hears a person's confession (ii) An admission, by a Christian, of wrong-doing. (iii) A particular official statement (or profession) of faith.

confirmation A ceremony held when a child is old enough to confirm the promises made on their behalf at baptism.

consecration The act of blessing of the bread and wine, at which point God becomes present.

creed A statement of beliefs.

crucifixion The Roman method of executing criminals and traitors by fastening them to a cross until they died. Used to execute Jesus Christ.

dedication A service of welcoming a new baby into a Christian community.

denomination A section of the Christian Church.

devotion Worship of a person, event or place that has special significance.

Easter The Christian festival to commemorate the resurrection of Christ from the dead.

Ecumenical A movement that brings different churches together.

Eucharist Thanksgiving service celebrating the sacrificial death and resurrection of Jesus Christ; also known as Holy Communion or Mass.

evangelist Someone who proclaims the word of God as described in the scriptures.

Father One person of the threefold nature of God; one of the Trinity.

festival A special occasion in the Church when an important event is celebrated.

Free Church Non-conformist Church, free from State control.

godparents People chosen by parents to support a child at their baptism and help bring them up to follow a Christian way of life.

Good Friday The Friday in Holy Week, commemorating the day when Christ was executed.

gospel One of the four books of the New Testament that relate the stories of Jesus in his life on Earth.

Heaven The place, or state, in which souls will be united with God after death.

Hell The place, or state, in which souls will be separated from God after death.

Holy Spirit One person of the threefold nature of God; one of the Trinity.

Holy Week The week before Easter, when Christians recall the last week of Christ's life on Earth.

host The special wafer-thin bread which represents Jesus' body in Holy Communion.

hymns Religious songs used during services; the words often being taken from the Bible.

incarnation The doctrine that God took human form in Jesus Christ.

infant baptism A ceremony to welcome a baby into the Church; godparents promise to help bring up the child in the Christian faith.

Jesus of Nazareth The central figure of Christian history and devotion. The second person of the Trinity.

lectern The desk in a church from which sacred texts are read.

lectionary A special book of the readings to be used in Mass.

Lent The 40 days leading up to Easter.

liturgy The service of worship in a religious ceremony according to a prescribed ritual.

Lord Title used for Jesus to express his divine lordship over people, time and space.

Lutheran A Protestant Church, named after Martin Luther.

Mary The Virgin Mary, Mother of Christ, Mother of God.

Mass A name for the eucharist.

Maundy Thursday The Thursday in Holy Week, commemorating the Last Supper.

Methodist A Christian who belongs to the Methodist Church, a Free Church founded by John Wesley in the 18th Century.

New Testament Collection of 27 books forming the second section of the Canon of Christian Scriptures.

non-conformist Protestant Churches which became separated from the established Church of England in the 17th Century.

non-conformists Christian groups which broke away from the Church of England.

Old Testament That part of the Christian Scriptures which the Church shares with Judaism, comprising 39 books covering the Hebrew Canon (and in the case of certain denominations, some additional books).

orthodox A Church within the Eastern tradition of Christianity. It is also used to mean someone who follows the teaching of their Church (in which case it is written as 'orthodox').

Palm Sunday The Sunday before Easter, commemorating the entry of Christ into Jerusalem.

Paschal Anything to do with the Christian feast of Easter.

passion The sufferings of Jesus Christ, especially in the time leading up to his crucifixion.

patriarch The title for principal Eastern Orthodox bishops. Also used for early Israelite leaders such as Abraham, Isaac and Jacob.

penance Part of the Sacrament of Reconciliation.

Pentecost Fifty days after Easter, Catholics celebrate the birth of the Church as they commemorate the arrival of the Holy Spirit.

pilgrimage A journey to a special place associated with, usually, a religious event, person or particular type of worship.

Pope The Bishop of Rome, head of the Roman Catholic Church.

prayer Speaking to God.

Protestant (i) The part of the Christian Church which separated from the Roman Catholic and Orthodox Churches in the 16th Century when their members professed (or 'protested', hence the name) the centrality of the Bible and other beliefs. (ii) Members of Protestant Churches.

Quaker A member of the Religious Society of Friends, a movement founded in the 17th Century by George Fox and which does not fit easily within the three main traditions of Christianity.

Reformation The historical event that led to the separation of Catholicism from other parts of the Western (not Eastern Orthodox) tradition of Christianity in the 16th Century.

resurrection The belief that Christ rose from the dead after his execution.

Roman Catholic The part of the Church owing loyalty to the Bishop of Rome, as distinct to the Orthodox and Protestant traditions; often abbreviated to 'Catholic'.

rosary String of prayer beads.

Sabbath The day of rest.

sacrament An outward visible sign of an inward spiritual grace.

sacred Holy; something or somewhere with particular religious meaning.

schism The technical term for the split between the Eastern and Western traditions of Christianity in 1054 CE.

scripture A general name for the sacred writings of Christianity and other faiths.

secular Having a view of the world which is not religious.

sermon Religious talk given by priest or minister during services.

sin (i) An act of rebellion against the known will of God, (ii) the general condition of all humans at birth of sinfulness, or lack of holiness, into which human beings are born, arising from Adam's sin in the garden of Eden.

Son One person of the threefold nature of God; one of the Trinity.

translation The process by which the original words of the Bible's authors were converted into the vernacular.

Testament Translated, this means 'promise' and refers to the promise God made to his people as described in the first part of the Bible.

Triduum The three important ceremonies of Easter: the Maundatum on Holy Thursday, the Good Friday liturgy and the Vigil Mass on Easter Saturday.

Trinity Three persons in one God; doctrine of the threefold nature of God – Father, Son and Holy Spirit.

Vatican The residence of the Pope in Rome and the administrative centre of the Roman Catholic Church. The main building of the Vatican is St Peter's Basilica, built on the traditional site of St Peter's tomb.

vernacular The ordinary language of the people reading the Bible.

Virgin Birth The doctrine of the miraculous conception of Jesus Christ by the Virgin Mary through the power of the Holy Spirit and without the agency of a human father.

worship Pay respect or homage to someone or something.

Index